Platform Power and Libraries

Number 3 in the Series on Critical Information Organization in LIS,
Violet Fox and Kelsey George Sigle, Series Editors.

Platform Power and Libraries

Edited by
Christine F. Smith

Library Juice Press
Sacramento, CA

Copyright 2025

Published in 2025 by Litwin Books.

Litwin Books
PO Box 188784
Sacramento, CA 95818

http://litwinbooks.com/

This book is printed on acid-free paper.

Publisher's Cataloging in Publication
    Names: Smith, Christine, editor.
    Title: Platform power and libraries / edited by Christine Smith.
    Description: Sacramento, CA : Litwin Books, 2025. | Includes bibliographical references and
        index.
    Identifiers: LCCN 2025934806 | ISBN 9781634001564 (acid-free paper)
    Subjects: LCSH: Information society. | Electronic information resources – Political aspects. |
        Libraries – Political aspects. | Information technology – Social aspects. | Internet – Social
        aspects. | Libraries and society.
    Classification: LCC HM851.P53 2025 | DDC 302.23--dc23
    LC record available at https://lccn.loc.gov/2025934806

Contents

vii   Preface
Christine F. Smith

ix   Acknowledgments

1   Platform Power and Libraries
Christine F. Smith

27   Challenging Digital Property Regimes in Public Libraries
Elena Rowan

63   Entanglements: How Academic and Commercial Streaming Film Platforms are Reshaping Academic Libraries, Research, and Learning
lisa Hooper

87   Digital Heritage after Platformisation: Double Binds at Two Legal Deposit Libraries
Kieran Hegarty

115   The Closed-Loop: Academic Publication and the Data Surveillance Conundrum
Jordan S. Sly and Joseph A. Koivisto

145   Biographies

147   Index

Preface

Christine F. Smith

> One of the strangest things about capitalism is [that] the capitalists...do not really control it. They are like characters in a play. They have a role to perform...Fortunately, there are communities actively engaged in constructing an alternative...an internet where the people rule.[1]

While working my way through the library and information studies (LIS) sphere, I have had the opportunity to work in academic, public and school libraries, not-for-profits, and even corporate institutions. My preceding background in communication studies has allowed me to see the LIS field with nuances that have informed my practice. It is through this lens of communication and media studies as well as that of political economics and critical LIS, that one can see that most, if not all, library professionals find ourselves as actors in the capitalist world in which we live.[2] As such, while specific examples will be used throughout this book, this book is not intended to be

---

1 Ben Tarnoff, *Internet for the People: The Fight for Our Digital Future*. (London ; New York: Verso, 2022), 36-37.

2 Howard Zinn, "Secrecy, Archives and the Public Interest." *The Midwestern Archivist* 2, no. 2 (1977) 14-26 https://www.howardzinn.org/wp-content/uploads/2021/12/Secrecy_Archives_Public-Interest_MA02_2.pdf.; Michael H. Harris, "State Class and Cultural Reproduction: Toward a Theory of Library Service in the United States." *In Advances in Librarianship*, 14 (New York: Academic Press, 1986), 211–252.

a critique of specific individuals or organizations, rather it is a critique of the reality in which we live.

Because of this capitalist reality, and as expressed by librarians[3] for many years, it is imperative that library workers take a meta reflexive[4] approach to our practice. It is essential that we interrogate our positionality, analyse our institutions, and explore where libraries sit within the world. Whether that be the world of cultural institutions or GLAM (galleries, libraries, archives, and museums), of academia or the "academic-military-industrial complex,"[5] or of "the media-technology-military-industrial complex,"[6] we need to, as individuals, bring a critical light to the systems and structures in which we—whether consciously or unconsciously—play a part.[7] Even if we did not make them, we have a responsibility to know how and why they were made. What power structures do our work perpetuate? And, as our world becomes platform-laden, how do these platforms, and our professional engagement with them, further perpetuate these powers.

---

3   Zinn, "Secrecy."; Harris, "State."; Callan Bignoli, Sam Buechler, Deborah Caldwell, and Kelly McElroy, "Resisting Crisis Surveillance Capitalism in Academic Libraries." *Canadian Journal of Academic Librarianship* 7 (December 2021): 1–25. https://doi.org/10.33137/cjalrcbu.v7.36450. Stephen E. Bales and Lea Susan Engle, "The Counterhegemonic Academic Librarian: A Call to Action." *Progressive Librarian*, no. 40 (Fall/Winter 2012), 16–40.

4   Margaret S. Archer, *Making Our Way through the World: Human Reflexivity and Social Mobility*. (Cambridge, UK: Cambridge University Press, 2007).

5   ShinJoung Yeo, *Behind the Search Box: Google and the Global Internet Industry*. (Urbana: University of Illinois Press, 2023), 24.

6   Justin Schlosberg, *Media Ownership and Agenda Control: The Hidden Limits of the Information Age. Communication and Society*. (New York London: Routledge, 2017), 116.

7   Winnie Soon and Pablo R Velasco, "(De)Constructing Machines as Critical Technical Practice." *Convergence* 30, no. 1 (February 1, 2024): 116–141. https://doi.org/10.1177/13548565221148098.

Acknowledgments

Smith

Thank you to the chapter authors, series editors, and anonymous peer reviewers without whom this work would not be possible. Thanks as well to my parents for their guidance throughout life, and to Kayla, Daniel, and Jack for your love and support.

Rowan

This endeavor would not have been possible without the generosity of my research participants. I am forever grateful for their kind words, support, and willingness to share their thoughts and knowledge with me. I am also grateful for the support of my supervisor Dr. Chris Hurl and subject librarian Susie Breier, for their ongoing advice and encouragement, and to Christine Smith, for the opportunity to discuss and share my research.

Hooper

Gratitude to family and colleagues for creating the time and space to write this paper. Sincere thanks to my colleagues Katherine K. Hicks and Kay P. Maye for their valuable input.

Hegarty

Thank you to the current and former staff of the National Library of Australia (NLA) and the State Library of New South Wales (SLNSW), who generously shared their experiences and allowed me to be a guest at the library throughout 2021. Special thanks to Paul Koerbin and Russell Latham at the NLA and Sean Volke from the SLNSW for generously sharing their work with me and keeping me up-to-date on the challenges of collecting social media after I finished my fieldwork. Research for this chapter was supported by the Australian Research Council through grant LP170100222.

Sly & Koivisto

Thank you to our allies, vocal supporters, and comrades in the University of Maryland libraries and in our wider UMD research community and the open-minded library and campus administrators who have supported our work in this area. Most specifically we would like to thank Daniel Mack, Adriene Lim, and Michael Dougherty for their ongoing encouragement. We would also like to thank the organizers of the Charleston Conference for allowing our early presentation of this work and Christine Smith, the editor of this book, for allowing us space to explore our ideas further and in the company of other interesting works.

Platform Power and Libraries

Christine F. Smith

Capitalism

The foundations of platform power are steeped in capitalism.[1] Across many disciplines in the humanities and social sciences myriad texts analyse these foundations via explorations of "digital capitalism"[2] and "surveillance capitalism."[3] While much research is done on the impact of capitalism on the masses, studies of the institutional impact of digital capitalism, in educational technology (edtech),[4] libraries,[5] healthcare, ener-

---

1 Nick Srnicek, *Platform Capitalism*. (Cambridge, UK ; Malden, MA: Polity, 2017).

2 Christian Fuchs, "Critical Theory Foundations of Digital Capitalism: A Critical Political Economy Perspective," *tripleC: Communication, Capitalism & Critique. Open Access Journal for a Global Sustainable Information Society* 22, no. 1 (2024): 148–96., https://doi.org/10.31269/triplec.v22i1.1454; Thomas Allmer, Sevda Can Arslan, and Christian Fuchs, "Critical Perspectives on Digital Capitalism: Theories and Praxis. Introduction to the Special Issue." *tripleC: Communication, Capitalism & Critique. Open Access Journal for a Global Sustainable Information Society* 22, no. 1 (2024), https://doi.org/10.31269/triplec.v22i1.1501.; Jathan Sadowski "When Data Is Capital: Datafication, Accumulation, and Extraction," *Big Data & Society* 6, no. 1 (2019). https://doi.org/10.1177/2053951718820549.; Dan Schiller as per Yeo, *Behind*, 26.

3 Shoshana Zuboff, *The Age of Surveillance Capitalism: The Fight for a Human Future at the New Frontier of Power*. (New York: PublicAffairs, 2019).

4 Janine Arantes, "Educational Data Brokers: Using the Walkthrough Method to Identify Data Brokering by Edtech Platforms," *Learning, Media and Technology* 49, no. 2 (2024): 320–133. https://doi.org/10.1080/17439884.2022.2160986; Laura Czerniewicz and Jennifer Feldman, "'Technology Is Not Created by the Sky': Datafication and Educator Unease," *Learning, Media and Technology* 49, no. 3 (2024): 428–41. https://doi.org/10.1080/17439884.2023.2206137.

5 Bignoli, et al. "Resisting."

gy, and more,[6] are also present. Despite the open future that once was anticipated by such technological innovations as the internet, continuous emphasis on profit margins over equity have led to a much different digital world than foreseen, one grounded in privatization, commodification, and extractivism.[7] Influx of technology, exacerbated by the COVID-19 pandemic, have further entrenched corporate power[8]—a reality that was predicted to occur by some, as global crises have long been mechanisms to further solidify the power elite's force.[9]

However, these mechanisms on their own are not fully to blame; to quote Steve Matthewman, "technology is neither society's driver nor the source of all problems; the issue is technology's integration into society. Technological development is distorted under capitalism because it is impelled by the logics of profit and domination."[10] For the purposes of this book, we are drawing distinct attention to the technology of platforms, specifically in relation to libraries. It warrants noting that, as technology, platforms are not the root of the issue. The deeper root is the hegemonic capitalistic orientation that, in the eyes of many practitioners, necessitates their integration, all the while extracting value from the individuals using them. Platforms lock users into a specifically curated suite of digital tools, algorithmically optimising the user's goal, while covertly surveilling and commodifying this data to

---

6   Yeo, *Behind*.

7   Tarnoff, Internet.; Yeo, *Behind*, 49.; Garry Robson, "Big Nihilism: Generation Z, Surveillance Capitalism, and the Emerging Digital Technocracy," *Information & Culture* 58, no. 2 (2023): 180–204.

8   Bignoli, et al., "Resisting."; Czerniewicz and Feldman, "Technology."

9   Brian Michael Murphy, *We the Dead: Preserving Data at the End of the World* (Chapel Hill: The University of North Carolina Press, 2022).

10   As cited by Sam Popowich, "'Ruthless Criticism of All That Exists': Marxism, Technology, and Library Work," In *The Politics of Theory and the Practice of Critical Librarianship*, edited by Karen P. Nicholson and Maura Seale, 39–66, (Library Juice Press, 2018). https://doi.org/10.7939/r3-26j6-5r32.

promote business interests of platform shareholders. While algorithms, like those embedded in platforms, do not necessarily change user behaviour, they do create extensive datafication and commodification of user behaviour thereby eroding user privacy.[11] Why then are they used so extensively? Because the landscape has changed to require their use to accomplish so many tasks; lack of platform use could effectively lock people out of whole professional and personal spheres. This is, in part, because "the Internet has become a new transnational marketplace and driving force for capitalist development and expansion" [12] where the existence of platforms "alters the geography of existing markets and generates a new terrain of competition and potential monopolization."[13]

Platforms

Before exploring further, we must first clarify: what is a platform? The definition of this term is contested among scholars. Those who opt for prescriptive definitions believe that "platform" should be used in a restrictive fashion for specific technological

---

11 Pascal D. König, "Two Tales about the Power of Algorithms in Online Environments: On the Need for Transdisciplinary Dialogue in the Study of Algorithms and Digital Capitalism," *Media, Culture & Society* 44, no. 7 (2022): 1372–82. https://doi.org/10.1177/01634437221111893.; Eric Hellman, "16 of the Top 20 Research Journals Let Ad Networks Spy on Their Readers," *Go To Hellman* (blog), March 12, 2015. https://go-to-hellman.blogspot.com/2015/03/16-of-top-20-research-journals-let-ad.html.; Dorothea Salo and Stephen Kharfen, "Ain't Nobody's Business If I Do (Read Serials)," *The Serials Librarian* 70, 1-4 (2016): 55–61, https://doi.org/10.1080/0361526X.2016.1141629.; Cody Hanson, "User Tracking on Academic Publisher Platforms." 2019 https://www.codyh.com/writing/tracking.html.

12 Yeo, *Behind*, 1.

13 Devika Narayan, "Monopolization and Competition under Platform Capitalism: Analyzing Transformations in the Computing Industry," *New Media & Society* 25, no. 2 (2023): 287–306, https://doi.org/10.1177/14614448221149939.

functionality.[14] Conversely, those opting for a more descriptive definition recognize that the initial use of the term has been co-opted from its origins and now, both in the public and in academe, has a broader meaning. In this descriptive approach, platforms come to mean technology serving to mediate between individuals or groups of individuals (e.g. students, library users, employees, news readers, etc.) and a private corporation, brokering user data for financial gain.[15] Schlosberg categorizes this mediation into some or all of the following roles: "provider...aggregator...portal...gateway...facilitator."[16] Gillespie argues that platforms serve a combination of computational, architectural, figurative, and political functions.[17]

This text will adopt the broader, descriptive use of the term platform, that of an intermediary. While potentially innocuous sounding, as mere venues of service rather than producers of content, the intentional choice of suppliers in using the term platform actually "speaks to the term's utility for companies eluding regulation by claiming neutrality instead of selectivity."[18] Indeed, platforms are neither innocuous nor neutral.[19] They are instead, as Nielsen and Ganter posit:

> deeply relational...based on their ability to attract end users and partners... [Their] power is...generative...exercised

---

14 Ian Bogost and Nick Montfort, "Platform Studies: Frequently Questioned Answers," UC Irvine: Digital Arts and Culture (2009), https://escholarship.org/uc/item/01r0k-9br; Tarnoff, Internet; Rebecca Giblin and Cory Doctorow, *Chokepoint Capitalism: How Big Tech and Big Content Captured Creative Labor Markets and How We'll Win Them Back* (Boston: Beacon Press, 2022).

15 Arantes, "Educational."; Aarthi Vadde, "Platform or Publisher," *PMLA* 136, no. 3 (2021): 455–62, https://doi.org/10.1632/S0030812921000341.

16 Schlosberg, *Media Ownership*.

17 Tarleton Gillespie, "The Politics of 'Platforms,'" *New Media & Society* 12, no. 3 (2010): 347–64, https://doi.org/10.1177/1461444809342738.

18 Vadde, "Platform," 456.

19 Gillespie, "Politics."

through socio-technical systems built by companies that draw many different third parties in by empowering them to do things that each of them value and want, while in the process leading them to become ever-more dependent on the platform in question, increasingly intertwined in highly asymmetric relations.[20]

One might argue that the problem then must lie in the existence of platforms themselves. However, it is more so the structure, or "hourglass-shaped market,"[21] in which platforms exist and that which they support. That is, if one were to permit the metaphor, it is not the players alone that are the issue, but rather the entire game itself.

Libraries

Like platforms, libraries do not exist in a vacuum. As locales of information exchange, and by and large due to public funding regardless of their type,[22] libraries are extensions of the state.[23] They have, therefore, long been venues fraught with power differentials as relational institutions caught in the confluence of stated professional ideals and hegemonic practice.[24] For example, in her work analysing the Library of Congress (LC), Adler

---

20 Rasmus Kleis Nielsen and Sarah Anne Ganter, *The Power of Platforms: Shaping Media and Society*, Oxford Studies in Digital Politics, (Oxford, New York: Oxford University Press, 2022), 1-2.

21 Giblin and Doctorow, *Chokepoint Capitalism*, 15.

22 Be they academic, school, public, legal, governmental, research, etc.

23 Bales and Engle, "Counterhegemonic."; Douglas Raber, "Librarians as Organic Intellectuals: A Gramscian Approach to Blind Spots and Tunnel Vision," *Library Quarterly* 73, no. 1 (2003): 33-53.; Harris, "State."; Wayne A. Wiegand, "The Structure of Librarianship: Essay on an Information Profession," *Canadian Journal of Information and Library Science* 24, no. 1 (1999): 17-37.

24 Bales and Engle, "Counterhegemonic."; Michael Quinn Dudley, "The Dialectic of Academic Librarianship: A Critical Approach." *Canadian Journal of Academic Librarianship* 1 (January 2016): 107–110, https://doi.org/10.33137/cjal-rcbu.v1.25580.

"draws attention to prevailing assumptions and approaches to managing information resources…and how such practices contribute to the cultural reproduction of state ideology" rooted in neoliberal, free-market business models.[25]

Capitalism, Platforms, and Libraries

Looking back towards the history of internet search as we know it today, we can see origins in publicly funded academic libraries and research institutions.[26] Whatever the initial ethical orientation, it is now clearly visible that there is a "commodification of search and the role of government in creating conditions for capital."[27] As a link in the information chain, libraries can be seen as targets in this "commodification of information" which turns "information into a capitalist commodity."[28] This trend is not brand new, nor is it surprising. Thirty years ago, in 1994, "Lievrouw…cautioned…about the potential for corporate interests to undermine democracy, realizing the growing presence of such interests in libraries and information systems. Over twenty years later," Adler notes in 2015, "we see significantly increased participation by private enterprises in American libraries."[29] Nearly a decade after Adler, we can see platformitization (also written "platformisation;" defined by Helmond as "the rise of the platform as the dominant

---

25 Melissa A. Adler, "Broker of Information, the 'Nation's Most Important Commodity': The Library of Congress in the Neoliberal Era," *Information & Culture* 50, no. 1 (2015): 27, https://doi.org/10.7560/IC50102.

26 Yeo, *Behind*, 21.

27 Yeo, *Behind*, 17.

28 Simon Barron and Andrew Preater, "Critical Systems Librarianship," in *The Politics of Theory and the Practice of Critical Librarianship*, ed. by Karen P. Nicholson and Maura Seale, (Sacramento, California: Library Juice Press, 2017), 101.

29 Adler, "Broker," 27.

infrastructural and economic model")[30] has been fully embedded into the global library landscape. While Lievrouw's cautioning may have been seen as coincidental foreshadowing by some, it is quite aligned with the actual industry rhetoric of the time. Writing one year after Lievrouw, Bill Gates penned in 1995 that "there are those...who think the Internet has shown that information will be free...Although a great deal...will continue to be free, I believe the most attractive information...will continue to be produced with profit in mind."[31]

Terminologically, the words "library" and "platform" have coexisted in the LIS field for at least a decade. Often, they are seen together when referring to "Library Services Platforms" (LSP), a term used first by Marshall Breeding in 2011 to differentiate unified, consolidated digital library service systems from their predecessor, Integrated Library Systems (ILS).[32] However, references to library platforms can be found predating Breeding's 2011 piece (see Figure 1). Thus, while LSPs do play a pivotal role in the discourse regarding libraries and platforms, it is important to note that they are not the *only* platforms to be discussed. Indeed, there are platforms that provide the infrastructure and applications to support library services,[33] but as platformatization has exploded in a multitude of industries, other library platforms also play a part in LIS (be they ebook platforms, database platforms or otherwise). Furthermore, libraries are

---

30 Anne Helmond, "The Platformization of the Web: Making Web Data Platform Ready," *Social Media + Society* 1, no. 2 (July 2015), https://doi.org/10.1177/2056305115603080.

31 As cited by Michael Dawson and John Bellamy Foster, "Virtual Capitalism," in *Capitalism and the Information Age: The Political Economy of the Global Communication Revolution*, ed. by Robert Waterman McChesney, Ellen Meiksins Wood, and John Bellamy Foster, (New York, NY: Monthly Review Press, 1998), 61.

32 Marshall Breeding, "Library Services Platforms: A Maturing Genre of Products," *Library Technology Reports* 51, no. 4 (2015).

33 Marshall Breeding, "The Power of the Platform," *Computers in Libraries* 36, no. 9 (2016), https://librarytechnology.org/document/22052.

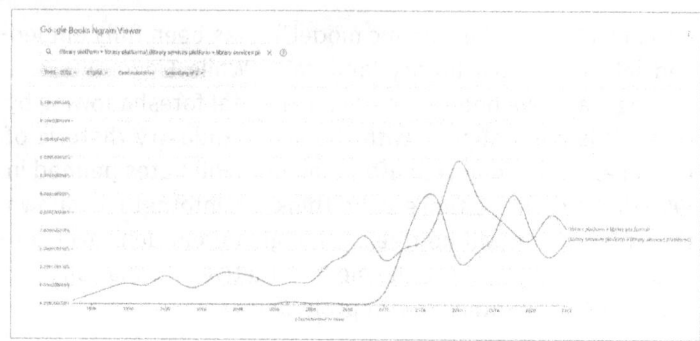

Figure 1   Screenshot of the tool Google Ngram Viewer (https://books.google.com/ngrams) and its search results for "Library Platform(s)" and "Library Services Platform(s).

increasingly finding themselves impacted by the platformitization of other markets as they attempt to uphold their core mission.[34]

Building on research in critical library systems studies, this book intends to draw to light the impact of platform power and libraries. We must first, however, situate platform power and libraries in the larger realm of platform studies. We will do so by looking at platforms in libraries through what Nielsen and Ganter call "the five most important aspects of platform power," that is:

1. The power to set standards...
2. The power to make or break connections...
3. The power of automated action at scale...
4. The power of information asymmetry...[and]
5. The power to operate across domains.[35]

---

[34] For example: Andreas Lenander Aegidius and Mads Møller Tommerup Andersen, "Collecting Streaming Services," *Convergence* (May 2024), https://doi.org/10.1177/13548565241253906; Nielsen and Ganter, *Power*, 189.

[35] Nielsen and Ganter, *Power*, 21.

"The power to set standards"

The relationality of platforms is a key element of their appeal. They can connect people and institutions to information, tools, products, and services to which they may not otherwise have access. This is often seen in libraries, as previously non-platformed tasks and tools (like cataloguing or reading a journal article) now take place in a platformed environment. However, there is distinct power in platforms as they alone can "set standards that others have to abide by if they want to be part of the…networks…and markets…platforms enable."[36] The most obvious of these standards is sole decision-making power over terms of use. That is, the power to decide how one is able to exist on a platform, what permitted use of data on a platform entails, and what gets someone kicked out or sued for breach of terms.[37] In libraries, these standards can manifest in such matters as deciding whether or not one is able to show a platformed film in class,[38] or whether platform content can be archived, or used in other contexts.[39]

Furthermore, as the platform industry has ballooned out of the United States (U.S.), it is important to recognize the weight of platform creators' worldviews and interests in their architecture of both technology and standards. That is, regardless of the location of the platform user or institution, standards

---

36 Nielsen and Ganter, *Power*, 21.

37 Giblin and Doctorow, *Chokepoint Capitalism*.

38 Christine F. Smith, Rumi Graham, and Eva Revitt.,"Leaps in Media Access & Reuse," (presentation at Canadian Association for Information Science Conference, Online, 2024). https://cais2024.ca/talk/24.smith/24.Smith.pdf; Christine F. Smith, "Lack of Collections as Data: Making Meaning out of the Films We Cannot See," *The Canadian Journal of Information and Library Science*, 47, no. 3 (2024). See also Chapter 3 by Hooper.

39 George Machovec, "Who Owns Bibliographic Metadata Created by Libraries?" *Journal of Library Administration* 63, no. 3 (April 3, 2023): 386–393, https://doi.org/10.1080/01930826.2023.2177928. See also Chapter 4 by Hegarty.

are often built with a U.S. lens in mind, as it is "the current capitalist imperial power."[40] Thus platform businesses do not just set standards within the platforms (i.e. products) themselves; such businesses also hold weight in impacting laws and other standards from being made or modified. An example of such intense global platform power can be seen in the work of Bannerman, et al. who track the communications between technology company lobbyists and public servants in the Canadian federal government.[41] Their findings, when read against those of the case studies in this text, can begin to highlight the impact that platforms can have both within and outside of virtual product "walls," as the laws they influence cause repercussions in libraries, as they have had in edtech[42] and other milieux.[43]

Beyond legal and technical standards, platform power can impact libraries in other, more covert ways. For example, while libraries and their employees may support equitable labour practices, platforms can obfuscate exploitative labour in their systems.[44] Additionally, platforms may breach normally upheld library privacy practices,[45] or charge libraries exorbitant

---

40 Yeo, *Behind*, 16.

41 Sara Bannerman, et al., "The Tech Lobby." (2024), https://thetechlobby.ca/.

42 Czerniewicz and Feldman, "Technology," 430.

43 Giblin and Doctorow, *Chokepoint Capitalism*, 144-145; Nielsen and Ganter, *Power*, 195.

44 Kristen C. Howard, "Digitization and Exploitation: Acknowledging and Addressing the Use of Exploitative Prison Labor by Libraries and Archives," *The Library Quarterly* 9, no. 3 (2023): 241–255, https://doi.org/10.1086/725070; Alexis Logsdon, "Ethical Digital Libraries and Prison Labor?" (presentattion at the Digital Library Federation Forum, Tampa, FL, October 15 2019) https://experts.umn.edu/en/publications/ethical-digital-libraries-and-prison-labor.

45 Erin Berman and Bonnie Tijerina, *The Ultimate Privacy Field Guide: A Workbook of Best Practices*, Chicago: ALA editions, 2023.; Laura K. Clark Hunt, Jennifer E. Steele, Janet L. Koposko, Josh Cromwell, and Tamatha A. Lambert, "E-Resource Librarians Perceptions on Library Patron Privacy," *The Journal of Academic Librarianship* 49, no. 3 (2023), https://doi.org/10.1016/j.acalib.2023.102704.

fees without transparency across the field.[46] Navigating such standards can be onerous or intentionally confounding for library employees.[47] Once clarified, platform standards may be found to be at odds with library best practices or librarian personal ethics and professional values, leading library workers to potential resignation and feelings of powerlessness.[48] Additionally, when LIS best practices do not support a platform's bottom line (like the ability, or lack thereof, to supply Machine Readable Cataloguing (MARC) records for resources acquired) such standards can create more work or prohibit work from being done. In sum, when platforms hold the power to set the standards, platforms have the final say.

"The power to make or break connections"

LIS literature has widely documented that the action of making connections between topics is grounded in the biases of those drawing the lines of connection. Whether classification, cataloguing, or other metadata, there is embedded therein the "power to control how and what we know, situating, stabilizing, and setting down the paths that can be travelled," write Allison-Cassin and Seeman, "it carries substantial weight, depth,

---

[46] Barbara Fister, "Liberating Knowledge: A Librarian's Manifesto for Change," *The National Education Association (NEA) Higher Education Journal, Special Focus: Radical Transformations,* (Fall 2010): 84-85.; Robert S. Fortner and Mark Fackler. *World Media Ethics: Cases and Commentary,* (Hoboken, NJ: John Wiley & Sons Inc, 2018), 9.

[47] Clark Hunt, et al., "E-Resource".

[48] Marc Zinaman, "Social Media Archiving in Practice: A Troubled Landscape in Review," *The Serials Librarian* (2024): 1–10, https://doi.org/10.1080/0361526X.2024.2367405; Czerniewicz and Feldman, "Technology," 430.; Nadja Schaetz, Emilija Gagrčin, Roland Toth, and Martin Emmer, "Algorithm Dependency in Platformized News Use," *New Media & Society,* (August 2023), https://doi.org/10.1177/14614448231193093; Nora A. Draper and Joseph Turow, "The Corporate Cultivation of Digital Resignation," *New Media & Society* 21, no. 8 (2019): 1824–1839, https://doi.org/10.1177/1461444819833331; Heather Howard, David Zwicky, and Danielle Walker, "Put Your Money Where Your Mouth Is: A Values-Based Evaluation Tool for Collections Decisions," *Collection Management* 48, no. 3 (2023): 165–77, https://doi.org/10.1080/01462679.2022.2150733.

and power."[49] Therefore, before discussing platform power in the making or breaking of connections in libraries, it must then be clarified that this text is not arguing that library-generated or -imposed structures are not biased. Quite the opposite; "theorists and practitioners from Sandy Berman (1993) to Hope Olsen (2002) have made clear that subject and classification standards are rife with problems."[50]

The power dynamic to be discussed here then is that, when outsourced to a third party, a platform, which may or may not have the same vision as those in the library,[51] the biases behind the metadata can be more easily glossed over, unquestioned, or concealed. This is as a result of the fact that "metadata's utility to aid search, discovery, retrieval, and interoperability means it is often neglected as textual in and of itself; its utilitarian nature obscures its tacit power."[52] Whether in discovery layers, resource databases, library purchasing interfaces, or otherwise, the way that information is organized by businesses serving libraries—the indexing, the content that is promoted as similar to one's readings, the relevance decisions that push some content to the top above others—holds immense

---

49 Stacy Allison-Cassin and Dean Seeman, "Metadata as Knowledge," *KULA: Knowledge Creation, Dissemination, and Preservation Studies* 6, no. 3 (2022): 1, https://doi.org/10.18357/kula.244.

50 Allison-Cassin and Seeman, "Metadata," 2.

51 Barron and Preater, "Critical," 95.; Jeremy Knox, "(Re)Politicising Data-Driven Education: From Ethical Principles to Radical Participation," *Learning, Media and Technology* 48, no. 2 (2023): 204, https://doi.org/10.1080/17439884.2022.2158466.

52 Allison-Cassin and Seeman, "Metadata," 3.

power.[53] It is often stated that libraries are not neutral, but when libraries rely on others to build connections on their behalf, the lack of neutrality deepens. When the decision to connect is left to platforms alone, it is they who have the power to "pick and choose" what connections to make or break.[54]

"The power of automated action at scale"

The magnitude of growing library platform amalgamation and reach provides key evidence of the impact of "the power of automated action at scale." In his 2020 edition of the annual Library Systems Report, Breeding writes that "the library technology industry has steadily consolidated over the last two decades, with the number of vendors narrowing at each round of acquisition."[55] Of the consolidations that year, Breeding notes that this "narrows the slate of competitors in an industry already offering few viable options for many libraries."[56]

---

53 Richard Wisneski, "I Can't Get No Satis-Searching: Reassessing Discovery Layers in Academic Libraries Journal of Web Librarianship," *Journal of Web Librarianship* 18, no. 1 (2024): 1–14. https://doi.org/10.1080/19322909.2024.2326687; Matthew Reidsma, *Masked by Trust: Bias in Library Discovery*, (Sacramento, CA: Litwin Books, 2019).; Lisa Romero, "Database Coverage for Communication Research: Implications for Collection Development," *The Serials Librarian* 83, no. 3/4 (2022): 233–260. https://doi.org/10.1080/0361526X.2023.2212019; Vadde, "Platform," 458; Andrew D. Asher, Lynda M. Duke, and Suzanne Wilson, "Paths of Discovery: Comparing the Search Effectiveness of EBSCO Discovery Service, Summon, Google Scholar, and Conventional Library Resources," *College & Research Libraries* 74, no. 5 (September 1, 2013): 464–88, https://doi.org/10.5860/crl-374; Sarah P. C. Dahlen, Heather Haeger, Kathlene Hanson, and Melissa Montellano, "Almost in the Wild: Student Search Behaviors When Librarians Aren't Looking," *The Journal of Academic Librarianship* 46, no. 1 (January 1, 2020). https://doi.org/10.1016/j.acalib.2019.102096; Simon van Bellen, Juan Pablo Alperin, and Vincent Larivière, "The Oligopoly of Academic Publishers Persists in Exclusive Database," *arXiv*, June 25, 2024. https://doi.org/10.48550/arXiv.2406.17893.

54 Tarleton Gillespie, "Platforms Intervene," *Social Media + Society*, 1, no. 1 (2015), 1, https://doi.org/10.1177/2056305115580479.

55 Marshall Breeding, "2020 Library Systems Report," *American Libraries Magazine* (May 1, 2020), https://americanlibrariesmagazine.org/2020/05/01/2020-library-systems-report/.

56 Breeding, "2020".

This narrowing of both depth and breadth of ownership means that a handful of private actors have the power to make decisions at scale that can impact libraries around the world. In today's libraries, private corporations maintain control over what resources are available and what are discontinued; they control which potential partners end up being close collaborators and which are locked out of collaborations all together. Should they choose to, they can effectively hold monopolies through mergers and acquisitions at the whims of their financial stakeholders. While platform providers may not have bad intentions in making these large-scale moves, it is the fact that they can make them to begin with that is cause for concern. As Giblin writes,

> Big Tech abuses monopoly power to deprive us of choice by limiting what we can buy, redirecting our searches to hide rivals' products, and locking us into ecosystems with technologies we can't alter without risking a lengthy prison sentence…[this] locking in users often begins with network effects—that phenomenon through which the value a user gets from a service increases with every additional user… when everyone's locked in, a better product or deal won't be enough to win them away.[57]

With the aforementioned global capitalistic orientation, we find ourselves in situations where these large-scale vendor automations cannot be undone with ease. As Smith and Appleton posit, "efficiency drives, including the move toward purchasing shelf-ready books from vendors, make customization at the local level increasingly difficult."[58]

---

57 Giblin and Doctorow, *Chokepoint Capitalism*, 36, 142, 144.

58 Trista Smith and Leo Appleton, "Addressing Classification System Bias in Higher Education Libraries in England," *Portal: Libraries and the Academy* 23, no. 4 (2023): 823.

"The power of information asymmetry"

With the power to make decisions about content, one holds the power to target certain content to certain users while withholding from others. In doing so, the power to control content decisions can quickly escalate to information asymmetry between different users. In platforms, powerholders are able to "operate as opaque black boxes where outsiders only see input and output on the basis of limited and biased data [while]... only the platforms are privy to how the processes work and have access to much more detailed data."[59] In this way, it is the platforms alone who become the ultimate gatekeepers, deciding what information to share, with whom, and when. Such polarity is contrary to basic democratic values as "education is a public good...an educated citizenry is an essential component of functional democracy,"[60] and "...in order for people to exercise their full rights as citizens, they must have access to...the broadest possible range of information...a communications system needs to be both diverse and open."[61]

When algorithms, content, and processes become obscured by platforms, it becomes easier for power holders to unquestioningly ground decisions for inclusion or exclusion in their own beliefs and values. In limiting decision makers and critiques to a smaller set of more uniform voices, platforms risk decreasing diversity and creating unease amongst their user

---

59 Nielsen and Ganter, *Power*, 21.

60 Natalie Greene Taylor, Karen Kettnich, Ursula Gorham, and Paul T. Jaeger, eds. *Libraries and the Global Retreat of Democracy: Confronting Polarization, Misinformation, and Suppression, Advances in Librarianship* 50 Bingley, UK: Emerald Publishing, 2022; Nailisa Tanner, "Knowledge for Sale: The Neoliberal Takeover of Higher Education, by Lawrence Busch," *Canadian Journal of Academic Librarianship* 4 (2019): 1–3. https://doi.org/10.33137/cjal-rcbu.v4.29644.

61 Graham Murdock and Peter Golding, "For a Political Economy of Mass Communications," *Socialist Register* 10 (March 1973): 21, https://socialistregister-com.lib-ezproxy.concordia.ca/index.php/srv/article/view/5355.

Figure 2　Screenshot of the introductory remarks of a redacted vendor's Spring 2024 Town Hall for customers.

communities.[62] Furthermore, as will be discussed later in this book, when the power of information distribution is asymmetrically assigned, platforms—especially those in libraries where access to information is primordial—risk the spread of mis- and disinformation.[63]

Additionally, as seen too often in libraries, information access is asymmetrically assigned for financial reasons. That is, while openness is essential "for people to exercise their full rights as citizens" and platforms tout the importance of said openness (even going as far as to cite renowned critics of capitalism in their business pitches, as illustrated in Figure 2), platforms can also prohibit access to this essential information

---

62　Czerniewicz and Feldman, "Technology," 438; Ana Stojanov and Ben Kei Daniel, "A Decade of Research into the Application of Big Data and Analytics in Higher Education: A Systematic Review of the Literature," *Education and Information Technologies* 29, no. 5 (2024): 5821, https://doi.org/10.1007/s10639-023-12033-8.; Thomas Poell, David Nieborg, and José van Dijck, "Platformisation," *Internet Policy Review* 8, no. 4 (2019): 3 https://policyreview.info/concepts/platformisation.

63　See Chapter 2 by Rowan.

unless sometimes exorbitant fees are paid.[64] This powerful asymmetry of information takes place at the expense of libraries, researchers, and citizens alike as access to cultural artifacts is withheld under the guise of "financial," "proprietary," or other reasons.

"The power to operate across domains"

Nielsen and Ganter provide the example of "data collected through a photo-sharing app...used to target advertising on a social network" to illustrate operating across domains.[65] But platform power need not be restricted to virtual domains. The magnitude of platform power can also be felt across industry domains (e.g. public libraries vs. academia) and sociopolitical domains, as platform power can be seen as a digital manifestation of globalisation's impact on libraries.[66]

This book provides texts from authors based in Canada, the United States, and Australia, each of whom are writing with their own inherent biases, and from their own positionality, global or otherwise. However, their arguments and findings can be found in similar scenarios around the world.[67] Connecting to "the power to set standards," it should not go unnoticed that globalisation of platforms increases their ability to function across multifold domains, allowing for operation around

---

64 Murdock and Golding, "Political Economy," 21.

65 Nielsen and Ganter, *Power*, 21.

66 Ruth Rikowski, Globalisation, *Information and Libraries: The Implications of the World Trade Organisation's GATS and TRIPS Agreements*, Oxford: Chandos, 2005; Robert Waterman McChesney, "The Political Economy of Global Communication," in *Capitalism and the Information Age: The Political Economy of the Global Communication Revolution*, ed. Robert Waterman McChesney, Ellen Meiksins Wood, and John Bellamy Foster, 1–26. New York, NY: Monthly Review Press, 1998.

67 See, for example, how Hegarty's chapter connects US platform power to Australian libraries.

the world, often at the expense of those already in marginalized situations.[68]

In the digital realm, there is an evidenced "rise of powerful intermediaries…creating online environments …of users who are surveilled to commercialize their attention and data."[69] Usage data, its extraction from libraries and those they serve, and later its monetization, is one of the LIS manifestations of "the power to operate across domains," as through data brokering, platforms can objectify information users' decisions for their own capital gains.[70]

Case Studies

The following chapters delve deeper into the pervasiveness of platform power in libraries by offering case studies exemplifying the aforementioned powers beginning with Rowan's discussion of the digital property regimes navigated in library ebook acquisition, management, and preservation. Grounding her research in the historical context of North American property regimes, Rowan's work looks at libraries, intellectual property, and cultural artifacts.

Beyond books, libraries have become environments where one can discover a myriad of information resources. The two chapters that follow highlight the increasing challenges that

---

68 Toussaint Nothias, "Access Granted: Facebook's Free Basics in Africa," *Media, Culture & Society* 42, no. 3 (2020): 329–48. https://doi.org/10.1177/0163443719890530; Czerniewicz and Feldman, "Technology," 430; Nora Schmidt, "The Privilege to Select: Global Research System, European Academic Library Collections, and Decolonisation." (Phd. thesisLund: Lund University, Faculties of Humanities and Theology, 2020), https://doi.org/10.5281/zenodo.4011296; Nielsen and Ganter, *Power*, 201.

69 König, "Two Tales," 1378.

70 Signe Sophus Lai, Victoria Andelsman, and Sofie Flensburg,"Datafied School Life: The Hidden Commodification of Digital Learning," *Learning, Media and Technology* 49, no. 3 (July 2, 2024): 371–387, https://doi.org/10.1080/17439884.2023.2219063; Nielsen and Ganter, *Power*, 203. See also Chapter 5 by Sly and Koivisto.

come with these new formats and bring to light the questions of how platform power impacts libraries in an information landscape where libraries are no longer just collecting printed works. First, in Chapter 3, Hooper highlights new challenges faced with acquiring moving images in a platform-laden world. She speaks to the "customer captivity" of streaming media platforms, as a select few hold dominant power in the library film distribution landscape, and goes on to elaborate on how library film media is one of the venues where disenfranchisement of the global south further facilitates barriers to culture and education.

In Chapter 4, Hegarty outlines the challenges faced by libraries whose mandates now encompass electronic legal deposit of social media posts. His work provides a forward-looking illustration of how business interests impact modern archiving. Through the concrete striking examples in his work, one can see the increased impact of platforms on collective heritage and cultural memory institutions.

Finally, this tome will close with Sly and Koivisto's chapter on the increasingly present coalescence of power in the scholarly realm. In this chapter, the authors speak more broadly about libraries, their place in academia, and how a perpetual cycle that privileges certain people and groups has taken hold via platformitization. This chapter will connect the information asymmetry of Nielsen and Ganter to Foucault's work in power distribution and extrapolate it to the information economy of today.

Through the case studies presented in this work, and the theoretical framing of this chapter, it is hoped that both those practicing and studying library and information can see the power that platforms now hold in libraries. In doing so, practitioners and scholars alike can make more informed decisions regarding the platform power and libraries.

Bibliography

Adler, Melissa A. "Broker of Information, the 'Nation's Most Important Commodity': The Library of Congress in the Neoliberal Era." *Information & Culture* 50, no. 1 (2015): 27. https://doi.org/10.7560/IC50102.

Aegidius, Andreas Lenander and Mads Møller Tommerup Andersen. "Collecting Streaming Services." *Convergence* 0, no. 0 (2024): 1-20. https://doi.org/10.1177/13548565241253906.

Allison-Cassin, Stacy and Dean Seeman. "Metadata as Knowledge." *KULA: Knowledge Creation, Dissemination, and Preservation Studies* 6, no. 3 (2022): 1-4. https://doi.org/10.18357/kula.244.

Allmer, Thomas, Sevda Can Arslan, and Christian Fuchs. "Critical Perspectives on Digital Capitalism: Theories and Praxis. Introduction to the Special Issue." tripleC: Communication, Capitalism & Critique. Open Access *Journal for a Global Sustainable Information Society* 22, no. 1 (2024): https://doi.org/10.31269/triplec.v22i1.1501.

Arantes, Janine. "Educational Data Brokers: Using the Walkthrough Method to Identify Data Brokering by Edtech Platforms." *Learning, Media and Technology* 49, no. 2 (2024): 320–333. https://doi.org/10.1080/17439884.2022.2160986.

Archer, Margaret S. *Making Our Way through the World: Human Reflexivity and Social Mobility*. Cambridge, UK: Cambridge University Press, 2007.

Asher, Andrew D., Lynda M. Duke, and Suzanne Wilson. "Paths of Discovery: Comparing the Search Effectiveness of EBSCO Discovery Service, Summon, Google Scholar, and Conventional Library Resources." *College & Research Libraries* 74, no. 5 (September 1, 2013): 464–88. https://doi.org/10.5860/crl-374.

Bales, Stephen E. and Lea Susan Engle. "The Counterhegemonic Academic Librarian: A Call to Action." *Progressive Librarian*, no. 40 (Fall/Winter 2012), 16–40.

Bannerman, Sara, et al. [2024] "The Tech Lobby." https://thetechlobby.ca/.

Barron, Simon and Andrew Preater. "Critical Systems Librarianship." In *The Politics of Theory and the Practice of Critical Librarianship*, edited by Karen P. Nicholson and Maura Seale. Sacramento, California: Library Juice Press, 2017.

Bellen, Simon van, Juan Pablo Alperin, and Vincent Larivière. "The Oligopoly of Academic Publishers Persists in Exclusive Database." *arXiv*, June 25, 2024. https://doi.org/10.48550/arXiv.2406.17893.

Berman, Erin, and Bonnie Tijerina. *The Ultimate Privacy Field Guide: A Workbook of Best Practices*. Chicago: ALA editions, 2023.

Bignoli, Callan, Sam Buechler, Deborah Caldwell, and Kelly McElroy. "Resisting Crisis Surveillance Capitalism in Academic Libraries." *Canadian Journal of Academic Librarianship* 7 (December 2021):1–25. https://doi.org/10.33137/cjalrcbu.v7.36450.

Bogost, Ian and Nick Montfort. "Platform Studies: Frequently Questioned Answers," *UC Irvine: Digital Arts and Culture* (2009). https://escholarship.org/uc/item/01r0k9br.

Breeding, Marshall."Library Services Platforms: A Maturing Genre of Products." *Library Technology Reports* 51, no. 4 (2015).

Breeding, Marshall "The Power of the Platform." *Computers in Libraries* 36, no. 9 (2016). https://librarytechnology.org/document/22052.

Breeding, Marshall "2020 Library Systems Report." *American Libraries Magazine* (May 1, 2020) https://americanlibrariesmagazine.org/2020/05/01/2020-library-systems-report/.

Clark Hunt, Laura K., Jennifer E. Steele, Janet L. Koposko, Josh Cromwell, and Tamatha A. Lambert. "E-Resource Librarians Perceptions on Library Patron Privacy." *The Journal of Academic Librarianship* 49, no. 3 (2023): https://doi.org/10.1016/j.acalib.2023.102704.

Czerniewicz, Laura and Jennifer Feldman. "'Technology Is Not Created by the Sky': Datafication and Educator Unease." *Learning, Media and Technology* 49, no. 3 (2024): 428–41. https://doi.org/10.1080/17439884.2023.2206137.

Dahlen, Sarah P. C., Heather Haeger, Kathlene Hanson, and Melissa Montellano. "Almost in the Wild: Student Search Behaviors When Librarians Aren't Looking." *The Journal of Academic Librarianship* 46, no. 1 (January 1, 2020). https://doi.org/10.1016/j.acalib.2019.102096.

Dawson, Michael and John Bellamy Foster. "Virtual Capitalism." In *Capitalism and the Information Age: The Political Economy of the Global Communication Revolution*, edited by Robert Waterman McChesney, Ellen Meiksins Wood, and John Bellamy Foster, New York, NY: Monthly Review Press, 1998.

Draper, Nora A. and Joseph Turow. "The Corporate Cultivation of Digital Resignation." *New Media & Society* 21, no. 8 (2019): 1824–1839. https://doi.org/10.1177/1461444819833331.

Dudley, Michael Quinn."The Dialectic of Academic Librarianship: A Critical Approach." *Canadian Journal of Academic Librarianship* 1 (January 2016): 107–10. https://doi.org/10.33137/cjal-rcbu.v1.25580.

Fister, Barbara."Liberating Knowledge: A Librarian's Manifesto for Change." The National Education Association (NEA) *Higher Education Journal*, Special Focus: Radical Transformations, (Fall 2010): 84-85.

Fortner, Robert S. and Mark Fackler. *World Media Ethics: Cases and Commentary*. Hoboken, NJ: John Wiley & Sons Inc, 2018.

Fuchs, Christian. "Critical Theory Foundations of Digital Capitalism: A Critical Political Economy Perspective." *tripleC: Communication, Capitalism & Critique. Open Access Journal for a Global Sustainable Information Society* 22, no. 1 (2024): 148–96. https://doi.org/10.31269/triplec.v22i1.1454.

Giblin, Rebecca and Cory Doctorow. *Chokepoint Capitalism: How Big Tech and Big Content Captured Creative Labor Markets and How We'll Win Them Back*. Boston: Beacon Press, 2022.

Gillespie, Tarleton. "The Politics of 'Platforms.'" I 12, no. 3 (2010): 347–64. https://doi.org/10.1177/1461444809342738.

Gillespie, Tarleton "Platforms Intervene." *Social Media + Society*, 1, no. 1 (2015) https://doi.org/10.1177/2056305115580479#.

Harris, Michael H."State Class and Cultural Reproduction: Toward a Theory of Library Service in the United States." In *Advances in Librarianship*, 14 (New York: Academic Press, 1986), 211–52.

Hanson, Cody. 2019. "User Tracking on Academic Publisher Platforms." 2019. https://www.codyh.com/writing/tracking.html.

Hellman, Eric. 2015. "16 of the Top 20 Research Journals Let Ad Networks Spy on Their Readers." *Go To Hellman* (blog). March 12, 2015. https://go-to-hellman.blogspot.com/2015/03/16-of-top-20-research-journals-let-ad.html.

Helmond, Anne. "The Platformization of the Web: Making Web Data Platform Ready." *Social Media + Society* 1, no. 2 (July 2015), https://doi.org/10.1177/2056305115603080.

Howard, Heather, David Zwicky, and Danielle Walker. "Put Your Money Where Your Mouth Is: A Values-Based Evaluation Tool for Collections Decisions." *Collection Management* 48, no. 3 (2023): 165–77. https://doi.org/10.1080/01462679.2022.2150733.

Howard, Kristen C. "Digitization and Exploitation: Acknowledging and Addressing the Use of Exploitative Prison Labor by Libraries and Archives." *The Library Quarterly* 9, no. 3 (2023): 241–55. https://doi.org/10.1086/725070

Knox, Jeremy. "(Re)Politicising Data-Driven Education: From Ethical Principles to Radical Participation." *Learning, Media and Technology* 48, no. 2 (2023): 1-2. https://doi.org/10.1080/17439884.2022.2158466.

König, Pascal D. "Two Tales about the Power of Algorithms in Online Environments: On the Need for Transdisciplinary Dialogue in the Study of Algorithms and Digital Capitalism." *Media, Culture & Society* 44, no. 7 (2022): 1372–1382. https://doi.org/10.1177/01634437221111893.

Lai, Signe Sophus, Victoria Andelsman, and Sofie Flensburg. "Datafied School Life: The Hidden Commodification of Digital Learning." *Learning, Media and Technology* 49, no. 3 (July 2, 2024): 371–87. https://doi.org/10.1080/17439884.2023.2219063.

Logsdon, Alexis. "Ethical Digital Libraries and Prison Labor?" Paper presented at the Digital Library Federation Forum, Tampa, FL, October 15, 2019. https://experts.umn.edu/en/publications/ethical-digital-libraries-and-prison-labor.

Machovec, George. "Who Owns Bibliographic Metadata Created by Libraries?" *Journal of Library Administration* 63, no. 3 (April 3, 2023): 386–93. https://doi.org/10.1080/01930826.2023.2177928.

McChesney, Robert Waterman. "The Political Economy of Global Communication." In *Capitalism and the Information Age: The Political Economy of the Global Communication Revolution*, edited by Robert Waterman McChesney, Ellen Meiksins Wood, and John Bellamy Foster, 1–26. New York, NY: Monthly Review Press, 1998.

Murdock, Graham and Peter Golding. "For a Political Economy of Mass Communications." *Socialist Register* 10 (March 1973): 205-234 https://socialistregister-com.lib-ezproxy.concordia.ca/index.php/srv/article/view/5355.

Murphy, Brian Michael. *We the Dead: Preserving Data at the End of the World*. Chapel Hill: The University of North Carolina Press, 2022.

Narayan, Devika. "Monopolization and Competition under Platform Capitalism: Analyzing Transformations in the Computing Industry." *New Media & Society* 25, no. 2 (2023): 287–306. https://doi.org/10.1177/14614448221149939.

Nielsen, Rasmus Kleis and Sarah Anne Ganter. *The Power of Platforms: Shaping Media and Society*. Oxford Studies in Digital Politics. Oxford, New York: Oxford University Press, 2022.

Nothias, Toussaint. "Access Granted: Facebook's Free Basics in Africa." *Media, Culture & Society* 42, no. 3 (2020): 329–348. https://doi.org/10.1177/0163443719890530.

Poell, Thomas, David Nieborg, and José van Dijck. "Platformisation." *Internet Policy Review* 8, no. 4 (2019): 1-13. https://policyreview.info/concepts/platformisation.

Popowich, Sam, "'Ruthless Criticism of All That Exists': Marxism, Technology, and Library Work." In *The Politics of Theory and the Practice of Critical Librarianship*, edited by Karen P. Nicholson and Maura Seale, 39–66. (Library Juice Press, 2018). https://doi.org/10.7939/r3-26j6-5r32.

Raber, Douglas. "Librarians as Organic Intellectuals: A Gramscian Approach to Blind Spots and Tunnel Vision." *Library Quarterly* 73, no. 1 (2003): 33-53.

Reidsma, Matthew. *Masked by Trust: Bias in Library Discovery*. (Sacramento, CA: Litwin Books, 2019).

Rikowski, Ruth. *Globalisation, Information and Libraries: The Implications of the World Trade Organisation's GATS and TRIPS Agreements*. Oxford: Chandos, 2005.

Robson, Garry. "Big Nihilism: Generation Z, Surveillance Capitalism, and the Emerging Digital Technocracy." *Information & Culture* 58, no. 2 (2023): 180–204.

Romero, Lisa. "Database Coverage for Communication Research: Implications for Collection Development." *The Serials Librarian* 83, no. 3/4 (2022): 233–260. https://doi.org/10.1080/0361526X.2023.2212019.

Sadowski, Jathan. "When Data Is Capital: Datafication, Accumulation, and Extraction." *Big Data & Society* 6, no. 1 (2019). https://doi.org/10.1177/2053951718820549.

Salo, Dorothea, and Stephen Kharfen. 2016. "Ain't Nobody's Business If I Do (Read Serials)." *The Serials Librarian* 70 (1–4): 55–61. https://doi.org/10.1080/0361526X.2016.1141629.

Schaetz, Nadja, Emilija Gagrčin, Roland Toth, and Martin Emmer. "Algorithm Dependency in Platformized News Use." *New Media & Society*, (August 2023). https://doi.org/10.1177/14614448231193093.

Schlosberg, Justin. *Media Ownership and Agenda Control: The Hidden Limits of the Information Age.* Communication and Society. New York London: Routledge, 2017.

Schmidt, Nora. "The Privilege to Select: Global Research System, European Academic Library Collections, and Decolonisation." Phd. thesis, Lund: Lund University, Faculties of Humanities and Theology, 2020). https://doi.org/10.5281/zenodo.4011296.

Smith, Trista and Leo Appleton. "Addressing Classification System Bias in Higher Education Libraries in England." *Portal: Libraries and the Academy* 23, no. 4 (2023): 819-841.

Smith, Christine F, "Lack of Collections as Data: Making Meaning out of the Films We Cannot See." *The Canadian Journal of Information and Library Science* 47, no. 3 (2024): 11-20. https://doi.org/10.5206/cjils-rcsib.v47i3.18988.

Smith, Christine F., Rumi Graham, and Eva Revitt. "Leaps in Media Access & Reuse." Presented at Canadian Association for Information Science Conference, Online, 2024. https://cais2024.ca/talk/24.smith/24.Smith.pdf

Soon, Winnie, and Pablo R. Velasco. "(De)Constructing Machines as Critical Technical Practice." *Convergence* 30, no. 1 (February 1, 2024): 116–41. https://doi.org/10.1177/13548565221148098.

Srnicek, Nick, *Platform Capitalism*. Cambridge, UK ; Malden, MA: Polity, 2017.

Stojanov, Ana and Ben Kei Daniel. "A Decade of Research into the Application of Big Data and Analytics in Higher Education: A Systematic Review of the Literature." *Education and Information Technologies* 29, no. 5 (2024): 5804-8531. https://doi.org/10.1007/s10639-023-12033-8.

Tanner, Nailisa. "Knowledge for Sale: The Neoliberal Takeover of Higher Education, by Lawrence Busch." *Canadian Journal of Academic Librarianship* 4 (2019): 1–3. https://doi.org/10.33137/cjal-rc-bu.v4.29644.

Tarnoff, Ben. *Internet for the People: The Fight for Our Digital Future*. London; New York: Verso, 2022.

Taylor, Natalie Greene, Karen Kettnich, Ursula Gorham, and Paul T. Jaeger, editors. *Libraries and the Global Retreat of Democracy: Confronting Polarization, Misinformation, and Suppression*. Advances in Librarianship 50. Bingley, UK: Emerald Publishing, 2022.

Vadde, Aarthi, "Platform or Publisher." PMLA 136, no. 3 (2021): 455–462. https://doi.org/10.1632/S0030812921000341.

Wiegand, Wayne A. "The Structure of Librarianship: Essay on an Information Profession," *Canadian Journal of Information and Library Science* 24, no. 1 (1999): 17-37.

Wisneski, Richard, "I Can't Get No Satis-Searching: Reassessing Discovery Layers in Academic Libraries Journal of Web Librarianship." *Journal of Web Librarianship* 18, no. 1 (2024): 1–14.; https://doi.org/10.1080/19322909.2024.2326687.

Yeo, ShinJoung. *Behind the Search Box: Google and the Global Internet Industry*. Urbana: University of Illinois Press, 2023.

Zinaman, Marc. "Social Media Archiving in Practice: A Troubled Landscape in Review." *The Serials Librarian* (2024): 1–10. https://doi.org/10.1080/0361526X.2024.2367405.

Zinn, Howard."Secrecy, Archives and the Public Interest." *The Midwestern Archivist* 2, no. 2 (1977) 14-26 https://www.howardzinn.org/wp-content/uploads/2021/12/Secrecy_Archives_Public-Interest_MA02_2.pdf.

Zuboff, Shoshana. *The Age of Surveillance Capitalism: The Fight for a Human Future at the New Frontier of Power*. New York: PublicAffairs, 2019.

Challenging Digital Property Regimes in Public Libraries

Elena Rowan

The research in this chapter investigates the power relationships between libraries and digital lending platforms, examines how librarians and library advocates across North America fight for fair digital lending, and argues that the current digital lending model constitutes a new digital property regime governing libraries. Original data was collected and reviewed from interviews with nineteen library-affiliated individuals. The interviews reveal that librarians find platforms untrustworthy actors in the space and highlight key factors including platform content, digital ownership, ongoing preservation, and patron privacy.

Introduction

In spring 2021, library platform Hoopla came under scrutiny for hosting Holocaust-denying titles in their library database.[1] Following the wake of the media story, Springfield Public Library's staff launched a thorough investigation of their own Hoopla holdings and realized holocaust-denying titles were

---

1   Maureen Amyot et al., "Hoopla Has a Content Problem: Here's How To Fix It," *Library Journal*, August 23, 2022, https://www.libraryjournal.com/story/hoopla-has-a-content-problem-heres-how-to-fix-it-backtalk.

not the only questionable content. Springfield Public Library is an anonymized name for a North American library within a diverse suburban area with over 500,000 visitors last year. Sarah Johnson, the Head of Collections at Springfield Public Library, discovered that her Hoopla collection contained materials that did not meet collection standards, including books with medical misinformation, works containing extreme conspiracy theories, and guides on how to make weapons.[2]

Sarah and the team at Springfield were distraught—these books were accessible for their community to read. Sarah said they wrote to, and had meetings with, representatives at Hoopla where she asked to see Hoopla's collection development policy.[3] When it was finally sent to her, she realised it was nowhere near the quality of her own library's collection development policy.[4] Hoopla's policy did not require professional review of the books in their collection, misclassified scientific literature, and, according to Sarah, contributed to the growing problem of misinformation.[5]

Worryingly, while ebooks about conspiracy theories can easily be debunked and removed, content like erotica and fiction for mature audiences falls on the edge of what Springfield's collections development would normally include. The library does not buy a lot of this content and relies heavily on positive professional reviews to determine quality before making a purchase for their collection. This kind of due diligence is difficult to do with Hoopla. In their review, Sarah and her team also found in the Hoopla database erotica that she worries about. As she said in an interview:

---

[2] Sarah Johnson (anonymized librarian) in discussion with the author, November 2023.
[3] Johnson, discussion.
[4] Johnson.
[5] Johnson.

When we do purchase print erotica, [that] is because it's been positively reviewed. Part of why we need to do that is if it's ever challenged. Librarians at the moment are being accused of being pornographers and pedophiles, by people who just don't want their kids reading books about gay kids. I cannot even imagine the firestorm that would happen if a child accidentally accessed a horrible porno book through Hoopla, brought to you by Springfield Public Library.[6]

Sarah alerted Hoopla of her concerns, and they responded that 'kids mode' would fix the issue,[7] an answer that clearly demonstrates a divide between the goals of the platform to supply content and the goals of the library to serve as a public good. This lack of concern for the situation facing libraries and misunderstanding of the gravity of the situation permeated the conversations between Sarah and Hoopla and continues to cloud their relationship as they continue to review the books in the collection, title by title, to try to ensure the materials their patrons can access meet their library's standards.[8]

Sarah and her team are not the first librarians to have issues with library lending platforms.[9] Their story is just one example of how librarians are losing control of their digital library collections. Many of the emerging threats facing libraries are based on the fear and uncertainty inherent in this new property regime where libraries are resigned to licensing instead of owning the ebooks in their collections. This new property regime, where ownership of digital materials has been

---

6   Johnson.

7   Johnson.

8   Johnson.

9   Library Freedom Project, "We Demand Accountability from Hoopla Digital and OverDrive Regarding the Platforming of Fascist...," *Medium* (blog), March 3, 2022, https://libraryfreedom.medium.com/we-demand-accountability-from-hoopla-digital-and-overdrive-regarding-the-platforming-of-fascist-c47c88e62ddc.

supplanted by perpetual licensing of materials, means that libraries must pay and repay for products in perpetuity, losing their central role as preservers of content for the public good.[10]

This research investigates how librarians navigate a world where library lending platforms exert so much power, how the library's role as a lender has changed with digital material lending, and how librarians advocate for their continued ability to lend books and fight for control of their collections. The role of the library in a digital, platform-mediated world is changing, which raises the following questions: Is the library's core mission being undercut by publishers and platforms? What is the new role of libraries and librarians in this new property regime? How are librarians fighting for their rights?

Platforms like Hoopla and OverDrive, with their lending application Libby, are contributing to the emergence of a new property regime governing libraries' digital collections, where platforms have enabled publishers to retain an inordinate amount of control over the books they publish. As for-profit businesses acting as third-party intermediaries, these platforms wield enormous power over libraries' digital collections.

Under the emerging property regime, contract law in many regions means that librarians may not be able to preserve ebooks (both audiobooks and/or digital content) or protect patron privacy, and in some cases, they are losing their ability to manage collection development altogether.[11] The rise of library digital platforms means that platforms are providing

---

10   Canadian Urban Institute Institut Urbain du Canada, "OVERDUE: The Case for Canada's Public Libraries," October 2023, https://canurb.org/publications/overdue/; Sarah Lamdan et al., "The Anti-Ownership Ebook Economy: How Publishers and Platforms Have Reshaped the Way We Read in the Digital Age," *SSRN Electronic Journal*, 2023, https://doi.org/10.2139/ssrn.4511975; Knowledge Rights 21, "A Position Statement from Knowledge Rights 21 on eBooks and eLending," May 2022, https://www.knowledgerights21.org/wp-content/uploads/2022/10/eBookPositionPaper150522.pdf.

11   Amyot et al., "Hoopla."

search, content delivery, and increasingly, curation of digital content for patrons on behalf of libraries, with less and less involvement from libraries themselves.[12] This is true across the spectrum of libraries, to varying degrees, from academic to public to school libraries.

This chapter will focus on the emerging power dynamics in the American and Canadian English-language library ebook licensing system. Using OverDrive and Hoopla as two descriptive case studies, this chapter will specifically examine the role of library lending platforms, or 'platforms,' and their relationship and tensions with libraries, making a case for the change not just as a marketplace, but as a new property regime. Though this work speaks explicitly to issues in North America, these issues are also experienced by libraries and librarians worldwide in many language markets.[13]

Major academic works in the social sciences, outside of library information sciences and critical librarianship studies, have generally examined public libraries as physical infrastructure, missing the emerging importance of the digital library.[14] However, more study by sociologists and the broader social sciences is greatly needed. The major library platforms are owned and operated by private corporate entities. These

---

[12] Further scholarship on the topic of digital platforms and the politics of search can be found in Safiya Umoja Noble's *Algorithms of Oppression*, Catherine D'Ignazio and Lauren F. Klein's *Data Feminism*, and Cathy O'Neil's *Weapons of Math Destruction*.

[13] Rafa Soler, "Library Associations across Europe Joint Call for Action on eBooks," *Knowledge Rights 21* (blog), April 24, 2023, https://www.knowledgerights21.org/news-story/library-associations-across-europe-joint-call-for-action-on-ebooks/; Rebecca Giblin et al., "Available—But Not Accessible? Investigating Publisher E-Lending Licensing Practices," *SSRN Scholarly Paper* (Rochester, NY, October 4, 2018), https://papers.ssrn.com/abstract=3346199.

[14] Eric Klinenberg, *Palaces for the People: How Social Infrastructure Can Help Fight Inequality, Polarization, and the Decline of Civic Life*, First edition (New York: Crown, 2018); Lisa M. Freeman and Nick Blomley, "Enacting Property: Making Space for the Public in the Municipal Library," *Environment and Planning C: Politics and Space* 37, no. 2 (March 1, 2019): 199–218, https://doi.org/10.1177/2399654418784024.

platforms, and their corporate owners, are consolidating power over ebook lending in an increasingly monopolised market. These platforms are restricting the abilities of librarians and libraries to own or source ebooks from providers with fair lending practices. As librarian advocates fight for their rights individually and organise collectively, sociological theories of power and property will be increasingly pertinent to advancing their cause for fair ebook lending. This research adds to ongoing research in library and information studies through a rich engagement with social science methodology to consider new digital materiality and a contemporary understanding of what it means to use and engage with digital infrastructures.

Methods

This research was conducted with twenty (n=20) individuals, including four public librarians, six members of library advocacy organizations (two in administrative positions), five academic librarians, three academics not working in library and information sciences, four library advocates not currently employed in libraries, and four digital content experts. Many participants held multiple roles, such as Sarah, for example, who is both a public librarian and a member of library advocacy organisations. Participants were initially contacted based on publicly available emails or LinkedIn connections. Snowball sampling methods were used, where previous participants shared study details with their networks to identify future participants.

All interviews were semi-structured, open-ended, and conducted over Zoom, of a length of between 35 and 190 minutes. Appendix A features the list of questions used as a guide during the interview. Ten of the participants were academically affiliated, and ten hold MLIS or equivalent degrees. Participants classified as digital content experts have no academic affiliation or MLIS degree. Four individuals have no academic affiliation but hold MLIS degrees—their words feature most heavily in this chapter, as they are the individuals who work directly in public libraries and/or with independent advocacy organisations not directly connected to universities. Of the public and academic librarians interviewed, all but one work in urban or suburban settings; the other individual works in a rural academic library. Overall, twelve of the participants identify as women and eight as men. As the industry is small, the names of some participants have been changed to protect anonymity. This requirement for anonymity limits the verifiability of the participants, which is a limitation of the study, but it does not change the validity of their statements.

As a snowball sample, this research is not likely to be representative of all librarians across North America. As the research is qualitative, the data is limited on its own in its ability to make generalizable conclusions to the industry. However, the librarians and advocates spoken to here do represent a group of librarians speaking up about the issues they see in their industry and among their fellow librarians. All participants, named or unnamed, speak in their personal, not professional, capacity.

New Property Regimes

Property is not a static concept, but is an ever-evolving, contested phenomenon exemplifying, as Nicholas Blomley puts it in his foreword to the edited collection "Contested Property Claims: What Disagreement Tells Us About Ownership" by Bruun et al., "a relationship between people, often mediated by institutions and caught up in asymmetrical power imbalances which lead to contestation and struggle."[15] Property regimes

---

15 Nicholas Blomley, "Foreword" In *Contested Property Claims: What Disagreement Tells Us About Ownership*, edited by *Ownership* Maja Hojer Bruun, Maja Hojer, Patrick J. L. Cockburn, Bjarke Skærlund Risager and Mikkel Thorup, xxi-xvi, (New York: Routledge, 2019).

are the ways in which societies organize their relationships between people with respect to the things they value[16] including arrangements which define rules, distribute rights, and delineate roles with respect to specific goods and are enabled by legal frameworks.[17] Questions of property are often confined to legal concerns about ownership and rights to access goods and services. Whereas legal theory is often specifically concerned with liberal definitions of ownership controlling private property and allocating scarce goods, other disciplines have investigated how everyday practice constructs and shapes property, highlighting how both theoretical law and the practice of law mutually constitute power relations.[18] Anthropologists, sociologists, and geographers have all attended to issues of property theory by analysing conflicts and transformations with and between the property regimes "through which societies order their relationships between people with respect to valued things."[19] In researching property as a connective thread that is constructed and shaped by everyday practice within, not outside of society, these scholars indicate the larger complications of digital property and digital materials that libraries are facing.

It is useful to understand libraries, digital materials, and their changing mandates through a mediated and contested property lens.[20] Most libraries in North America are mandated to serve their communities in a variety of ways, including the

---

16 Matthew Canfield, "Property Regimes," in *The Oxford Handbook of Law and Anthropology*, ed. Marie-Claire Foblets et al. (Oxford University Press, 2022), https://doi.org/10.1093/oxfordhb/9780198840534.013.23.

17 Luis F. Alvarez León, "Property Regimes and the Commodification of Geographic Information: An Examination of Google Street View," *Big Data & Society* 3, no. 2 (December 1, 2016), https://doi.org/10.1177/2053951716637885.

18 Canfield, "Property Regimes."

19 Canfield.

20 Freeman and Blomley, "Enacting Property."

provision of equal and universal access to information and free or low-cost services.[21] Many do this by buying and lending materials for the use of their members. Libraries can own items like books based on North American and European-origin legal understanding of books as things that can be owned or as items of property.[22]

Understanding property as a set of relations between owners, nonowners, and the state, and the difference between these types of property, is key to understanding the conflict surrounding the current ebook licensing debate. For the past century, tensions of ownership have permeated library collections as library books can uniquely be understood as both public and private property, the same as library space is both public and private.[23] Library books are collectively and institutionally owned for use by "the public," not by individuals.[24] In this sense, the new property regime being developed is based on a new organising set of relations, enabling certain possibilities, while closing off others.[25] In the case of library ebooks and other digital media, the new organising set of relations is around ebook platforms and the new possibilities are licensing of ebooks, closing off the opportunity to own ebooks.

The new digital property regime centred around licensing frameworks is at odds with the property regime otherwise understood to govern libraries' physical collections. Physical

---

[21] Michael Gorman, *Our Enduring Values: Librarianship in the 21st Century* (Chicago: American Library Association, 2000).

[22] Aaron Perzanowski and Jason Schultz, *The End of Ownership: Personal Property in the Digital Economy*, 2016, https://doi.org/10.7551/mitpress/10524.001.0001.

[23] Freeman and Blomley, "Enacting Property."

[24] Kyle K. Courtney and Juliya Ziskina, "The Publisher Playbook: A Brief History of the Publishing Industry's Obstruction of the Library Mission," Pre-print., 2023, https://dash.harvard.edu/handle/1/37374618.

[25] Maharawal et al., *Contested*.

books are owned and lent by libraries and governed by laws that dictate book lending, while ebook lending is based on leases and contracts between libraries, publishers, and platforms. This new property regime limits the library's capacity as owners, lenders, and preservers of digital resources.[26]

This new development is a considerable departure from the property regime governing physical library books. The law governing library lending of physical books is called the first sale doctrine in the United States,[27] and the doctrine of exhaustion in Canada.[28] While these doctrine are notably different, they both give libraries the right to buy, own, lend, circulate, preserve, resell, or even destroy books in Canada[29] and the United States.[30] Crucially, neither of these laws applies to digital materials, and they do not protect libraries from publishers inventing new markets to lease digital materials to recoup perceived losses in revenue. With the emergence of ebooks and audiobooks, publishers redefined usage models and prices, vastly increasing the prices and limiting access. Publishers tried to replicate their print business model, adhering digital rights management (DRM) software to digital files, making them 'exhaustible' and creating new usage models built upon first perpetual, then expiring licenses.[31] This led

---

26 Perzanowski and Schultz, *Ownership*.

27 Christina De Castell et al., "Controlled Digital Lending of Library Books in Canada," *Partnership: The Canadian Journal of Library and Information Practice and Research* 17, no. 2 (December 21, 2022): 1–35, https://doi.org/10.21083/partnership.v17i2.7100.

28 Debra Gold, "Research Guides: Copyright Information & Resources: Fair Dealing & Flowchart," accessed January 11, 2024, https://libguides.lakeheadu.ca/c.php?g=450304&p=3075879.

29 De Castell et al., "Controlled Digital Lending."

30 David R. Hansen and Kyle K. Courtney, "A White Paper on Controlled Digital Lending of Library Books," preprint (LawArXiv, September 24, 2018), https://doi.org/10.31228/osf.io/7fdyr.

31 Noorda Rachel and Inman Berens Kathi, "Digital Public Library Ecosystem 2023" (ALA, 2023).

to rapidly increasing costs for libraries. As demand for digital materials has increased, so too have the prices and restrictions imposed by publishers.[32] Over the past 20 years, this new reality has become an increasingly unsustainable situation for libraries.[33]

Under the new digital property regime, platforms are necessary intermediaries to engage with if a library wants to provide digital materials to its patrons. As the internet grows more commonplace in our everyday lives, libraries need to wrestle with the increasing importance of digital materials and the platforms that host them. Publishers and many authors understandably fear the free and easy ability to transfer materials over the internet, as their business models and livelihoods depend on being paid for the materials they produce. The creation of digital lending platforms makes sense from their perspective. However, this new property regime does not meet or account for the needs of the library, and by extension those who they serve, as it eliminates the possibility for libraries to preserve digital materials in their collections.

Ownership is a crucial and contested claim in digital library collections. Librarians interviewed for this research all highlighted the importance of owning the items in their collections as fundamental to their ability to operate as libraries. However, licensing digital materials under the current user models is expensive, exploitative, and unsustainable for libraries.[34] Critics of the myriad usage models for ebooks offered through licensing often cite the publishers as the problem, as they are the ones who set the price of ebooks. However, it should be

---

32 ALA and Joint Digital Content Working Group, "The Need for Change: A Position Paper on E-Lending," December 2020, http://www.ala.org/tools/librariestransform/working-group-libraries-and-digital-content.

33 Lamdan et al., "Anti-Ownership."

34 Lamdan et al., "Anti-Ownership."

understood that they are not the only ones exercising their power under this new property regime. As the place where libraries go to buy their books and publishers go to offer their licenses, platforms play a significant role as middlemen in this system.

This new licensing system, using platforms as intermediaries between libraries and publishers, has created a new digital property regime where publishers remain the sole property owners not just of the copyright but also of the physical ebooks. This new property regime also means that platforms are the sole distributors of this content, placing themselves in an increasingly monopolistic environment where they are indispensable to libraries wanting to offer ebooks to patrons and allowed to hold user data, check-out data, and other data that puts them in a position of power over essential library functions.

Platforms

Platforms exercise a "generative form of power through socio-technical systems built by companies."[35] In the case of this research, those companies are the platforms that provide ebook licensing options to libraries. These companies empower libraries who use them by offering services of value while in the process, leading those libraries receiving the platform's services "to become ever-more dependent on the platform in question, increasingly intertwined in highly asymmetric relations."[36] This relationship is fraught with tensions and conflicts.

Platforms are unique as a business model as they are, as Nick Srnicek argues in his book *Platform Capitalism*, centred on and

---

[35] Rasmus Kleis Nielsen and Sarah Anne Ganter, *The Power of Platforms: Shaping Media and Society*, Oxford Studies in Digital Politics (New York, NY: Oxford University Press, 2022).

[36] Nielsen and Ganter, *Power*.

designed to extract and use data to leverage themselves over other businesses. As Srnicek says:

> In essence, all are symptomatic of how twenty-first-century advanced capitalism is coming to be centred upon extracting and using a particular kind of raw material: data. And the business model which is adequate to this shift is the platform—digital infrastructures that intermediate between different groups. This is the key to its advantage over traditional business models when it comes to data, since a platform positions itself (1) between users, and (2) as the ground upon which their activities occur, thereby giving it privileged access to record them.[37]

The more librarians that use any individual platform, the more valuable that platform becomes within the library ecosystem, as patrons and librarians become increasingly familiar with one system. However, as Srnicek points out, this generates a cycle whereby more users beget more users.[38] This allows platforms to follow their 'natural' tendency towards consolidation and monopolisation of other businesses around them.[39] Moreover, their digital nature leaves few barriers to ever-increasing growth.[40]

Librarians are reliant on third parties to serve their community's needs. Libraries must work with numerous and diverse groups like governments, institutions, and businesses. They must constantly advocate for their needs, as their needs often conflict with their third-party providers' requirements to turn

---

37 Nick Srnicek, *Platform Capitalism*, 1 online resource (vi, 171 pages) vols., Theory Redux (Cambridge, UK ; Polity Press, 2017), EBSCOhost.

38 Srnicek, *Platform Capitalism*.

39 Srnicek.

40 Srnicek.

a profit. As a digital content expert with a library background said of the relationship:

> The reality of capitalism is that businesses have to do what's right for them. They have to figure out how to make money and sometimes those things are in conflict. Sometimes a shortcut will be necessary for the business to remain solvent, and that shortcut is not appreciated by the library. So, librarians often feel that vendors that supposedly serve them have not served them optimally. Sometimes they feel like they are getting ripped off.[41]

Under the digital property regime, many libraries and librarians use lending platforms to meet their needs. However, they still worry about the long-term consequences of becoming too reliant on these businesses. Libraries are becoming even more beholden to these platforms as patrons identify with the platforms rather than their library service.[42] This identification with the platform, not the library, is rooted in the platform's branding and design, leaving the library in a vulnerable position as an institution, with so many patrons using its services without realizing their financial origins and without knowing whether their library has licensed the item and it is hosted on a different platform. Platforms often put their concerns for patron loyalty ahead of the concerns of the libraries they serve. As a digital content expert says of the relationship:

> I do think that a lot of times these libraries do get taken advantage of, because they've got so many other things, they have to keep track of. They're in a stressful position, just by the very nature of what they do and who they are.[43]

---

41 Anonymous (digital content expert) in conversation with the author, December 2023.

42 Rachel and Kathi, "Digital."

43 Anonymous (digital content expert).

Platforms also act as chokepoints in the library lending ecosystem. Chokepoints, as described in Rebbeca Giblin and Cory Doctorow's *Chokepoint Capitalism*, are barriers to competition that businesses create that enable them to exploit their position in the market and capture value that could go to others.[44] Penguin Random House, HarperCollins, Hatchette Livre, Macmillan Publishers, and Simon & Schuster, also referred to as the Big Five publishers,[45] have generated vast economies of scale through their utilization of ebook licensing models on platforms like OverDrive and Hoopla as chokepoints to consolidate and grow their power in the library ebook market, ironically while being subjected to these same chokepoints themselves.[46] While publishers still control the production of books, both physical and digital, library platforms now control the channels through which people access digital books, and increasingly which books they can access, for how long, and when. As these platforms consolidate and grow, experts predict that the power of platforms over libraries will grow as well.[47]

Some platforms are removing curation control from librarians, which is increasingly costing libraries huge sums of money and taking up increasingly large percentages of their operating expenses and collection budgets.[48] Interviews with librarians like Sarah, Carmi Parker, and Michael Blackwell, which are

---

[44] Rebecca Giblin and Cory Doctorow, *Chokepoint Capitalism: How to Beat Big Tech, Tame Big Content, and Get Artists Paid* (Boston: Beacon Press, 2022) Overdrive.

[45] Jim Milliot, "Over the Past 25 Years, the Big Publishers Got Bigger—and Fewer," *PublishersWeekly.com*, accessed July 27, 2023, https://www.publishersweekly.com/pw/by-topic/industry-news/publisher-news/article/89038-over-the-past-25-years-the-big-publishers-got-bigger-and-fewer.html; Christine Wolf, "The Big Five Publishers: Who Are They?," Substack newsletter, *Writers' Haven* by Christine Wolf (blog), February 11, 2024, https://christinewolf.substack.com/p/the-big-five-publishers-who-are-they.

[46] Giblin and Doctorow, *Chokepoint Capitalism*.

[47] Rachel and Kathi, "Digital."

[48] Amyot et al., "Hoopla."

discussed below, all cite concerns over how much their collections are costing—at some small libraries, the costs are said to be 20% of the libraries operating budget. Indeed, even large libraries are facing issues increasing their collections—it is well-documented that leasing an ebook is significantly more expensive than buying a physical book.[49] In the author's own research for this chapter, she was given figures from her university's subject librarian that a single-user DRM controlled ebook license would cost $250CAD for the library, but $39 for the author to purchase themselves.[50] Many campaigns in Canada and the United States for fairness in library lending have been centred on this fact.[51] Though platforms claim this pressure comes from the publishers, platforms also take actions that hinder libraries, most especially in advocating for the championing and embracing of prevailing business models (licensing models) by authors and publishers,[52] instead of calling for a reworking of these problematic business models as many nonprofit advocacy organisations are advocating.[53]

OverDrive, the largest of the library lending platforms, was acquired first by Rakuten, then by private equity firm KKR in December 2021, for an estimated total of $1.185 billion USD.[54] Many research participants mentioned in interviews that OverDrive claims to operate on behalf of libraries. In a February

---

49 Rachel and Kathi, "Digital."

50 Elena Rowan, "Requesting Article," August 15, 2023.

51 Paul Whitney and Christina de Castell, "Trade eBooks in Libraries—The Changing Landscape," December 16, 2016, https://repository.ifla.org/handle/123456789/2028.

52 Steve Potash, "Thoughts from a Digital Advocate: Pursuing the Holy Grail of Library eBook Models," *OverDrive Steve* (blog), February 22, 2021, https://OverDrivesteve.com/pursuing-the-holy-grail-of-library-ebook-models/.

53 "Battle for Libraries," accessed January 30, 2024, https://www.battleforlibraries.com/.

54 Ed Nawotka, "Digital Book World: Startups Are Entering 'A New Age,'" *PublishersWeekly.com*, January 18, 2023, https://www.publishersweekly.com/pw/by-topic/digital/retailing/article/91317-digital-book-world-startups-are-entering-a-new-age.html.

2021 blog post, CEO Steve Potash wrote,"OverDrive has persevered for 20 years on behalf of libraries with authors and publishers to advocate for fair, flexible, and reasonable terms for library lending of popular titles."[55] However, as the largest and in many cases the only intermediary between libraries and publishers, it holds tremendous power over libraries. Many research participants regard trusting these platforms as an exercise in blind faith, as the level of control the platforms hold over libraries gives the libraries very little way to push back. OverDrive controls immense amounts of library information and patron data like time spent reading and number of books in an account.[56] Like other monopoly powers, platforms can exert influence on governments, crush competitors, hold back entire industries, and reorder the library ebook economy according to (their) whims.[57] Together with the Big Five publishers, the platforms have the power to influence the entire digital content lending system in many English-language countries. If they wanted to change the terms of the licenses, increase the prices of ebooks, or withdraw or change their catalogues to appease political groups, there is no institution or individual overseeing their actions.

As librarians like Carmi Parker told us, the contemporary ownership structure and emerging property regime is of huge concern to libraries like hers.[58] She is the ILS Administrator at the Whatcom County Library System, comprised of more than 14 libraries in northern Washington State, USA, and she discussed

---

55 Potash, "Thoughts from a Digital Advocate."

56 Daniel A. Gross, "The Surprisingly Big Business of Library E-Books," *The New Yorker*, September 2, 2021, https://www.newyorker.com/news/annals-of-communications/an-app-called-libby-and-the-surprisingly-big-business-of-library-e-books.

57 Giblin and Doctorow, *Chokepoint Capitalism*.

58 Carmi Parker, (librarian, Whatcom County Library System) in discussion with the author, November 2023.

her concerns about doing right by the taxpayers who fund their institution:

> I have a love/hate relationship with OverDrive. I think they are unusually good at creating a really positive end-user experience. Libby is a very good piece of software for being free. I mean, it's not free, we pay a lot for it, but the end user doesn't have to pay. They're a good partner in that way. I am not happy that they're no longer a private company. Because we license the content, these are assets that are not insured. I have no idea what we would do if OverDrive fell over and KKR decided not to pick it up again. So from a taxpayer due diligence standpoint, that's a bad thing. You wouldn't have a building full of books that wasn't insured. But that's exactly what we have, 80,000 books that, if something happens to OverDrive, there's no plan.[59]

Indeed, Sarah also voiced her concerns about OverDrive's power:

> (OverDrive's) Libby has a near monopoly on digital services in our state. If they went away, or decided to charge double, they could, and no one seems to be doing anything about it."[60]

While this research has not seen anything to indicate that OverDrive does not act as they state they do (i.e. on behalf of libraries), it is clear there is the potential for issues to arise and unclear to many of the librarians interviewed whether the platform is a friend or foe. Instead, the platform exists in a gray area with nuanced, complicated relationships that, for many, mean that platforms are untrustworthy actors in this new property regime. Librarians interviewed for this research

---

59 Parker, discussion.

60 Johnson, discussion.

are keenly aware that the interests of libraries and platforms are, at best, partially aligned but also increasingly in competition and even conflict.

Michael Blackwell, the director of the St. Mary's County Library in Maryland, USA, was an early adopter of ebooks under numerous platforms and leads the Readers First initiative, described as a movement to improve ebook access and services for public library users.[61] Michael highlighted some of the issues specific to OverDrive: their direct marketing to patrons, their increased costs, and their magazines' auto-subscribe feature.[62] Like most other librarians interviewed, he recognizes that their platforms work well for patrons, but not necessarily for libraries, as exemplified by putting unenforceable restrictions in their licensing terms and developing policies that cost libraries.[63] One such policy is their magazine auto-borrowing feature. While this feature is great for patrons, as it allows them to automatically borrow any magazine they mark as relevant to them, librarians have complained it is expensive and cannot be turned off.[64] Auto-borrowing features like this one may force the library to spend more money on magazines than they might have without the feature, as it is unclear if patrons read each magazine they have auto-borrowed.[65]

Another heavily critiqued feature of the OverDrive platform is the ability for patrons to simultaneously have more than one library card registered to their profile. OverDrive is excellent

---

61 Micah May, "A Conversation with Michael Blackwell on Maximizing Ebooks Access," *Digital Public Library of America* (blog), January 11, 2021, https://dp.la/news/qa-with-michael-blackwell-director-st-marys-county-library-maryland.

62 Michael Blackwell (library director, St. Mary's County Library and Readers First) in discussion with the author, January 2024.

63 Blackwell, discussion.

64 Blackwell.

65 Blackwell.

for patrons who move between cities frequently or whose cities feature many different library systems (like in the case of Montreal, Canada, where residents may have access to the municipal library system [the Bibliothèques de Montréal], the provincial Bibliothèque et Archives National du Québec, and other small private libraries). This has been a problem for large library systems like the New York Public Library, which has had to review its cardholder policies to ensure that it is serving its local audience. As Kathleen Riegelhaupt, the Director of eReading at the New York Public Library says:

> There are dedicated Reddit threads and online communities that advise people on how to get multiple library cards so that they can borrow ebooks from systems where they neither work nor live. Many users have learned how to game the system, at the expense of local communities. Users who have dozens of different library accounts simply go into the app and put a hold on the same book in different systems, and whichever one comes up first, they'll read. In the meantime, people in those communities face increased wait times and libraries make ebook acquisition decisions based on demand that isn't local and may not even be real.[66]

Furthermore, issues of privacy abound in digital lending platforms. Ebook usage data is robust and overlooked as a potential key issue with outsourcing patron data to platforms.[67] As a source of information on borrowers' habits, downloads, time spent reading, and much more, even with existing protections on physical books it is unclear to researchers how much data OverDrive is collecting, where it is going, and what

---

[66] Kathleen Riegelhaupt (Library Director of eReading at The New York Public Library) in discussion with the author, November 2023.

[67] Sarah Lamdan, *Data Cartels: The Companies That Control and Monopolize Our Information* (Stanford: Stanford University Press, 2022).

protections are being implemented on patron data held by platforms.[68] Platforms and publishers can use the power afforded to them in this digital property regime not only to extract exorbitant fees from libraries,[69] but to introduce mechanisms for tracking user behavior and conduct wider surveillance of reader habits.[70]

Additionally, ebooks licensed to patrons can be manipulated or removed according to the publisher's wishes.[71] In the growing context of pushback from politically motivated activist groups against physical libraries, librarians, and their collections, it is important to consider the ways that library ebooks can also be censored, altered, or erased. As evidenced by the 2009 case of Amazon removing the author George Orwell's books from Kindle libraries, ebooks are subject to erasure and censorship concerns at an increasing scale.[72]

Indeed, take the case of the platform Kanopy (a subsidiary of OverDrive),[73] told by one professional, Katelyn, who is not a librarian but has worked for a major United States library system for over 20 years.[74] When this library cancelled their service with Kanopy for budgetary reasons, Kanopy used the email list of that library's patrons to petition those patrons to

---

68 Lamdan, *Data Cartels*.

69 Gross, "Surprisingly."

70 Lamdan, *Data Cartels*.

71 Brad Stone, "Amazon Erases Orwell Books From Kindle," *The New York Times*, July 18, 2009, sec. Technology, https://www.nytimes.com/2009/07/18/technology/companies/18amazon.html.

72 Stone, "Amazon Erases Orwell Books From Kindle."

73 Andrew Albanese, "OverDrive to Acquire Kanopy," *PublishersWeekly.Com*, June 9, 2021, https://www.publishersweekly.com/pw/by-topic/industry-news/libraries/article/86608-OverDrive-to-acquire-kanopy.html.

74 Katelyn (library worker) in discussion with the author, December 2023.

ask for their library to keep their contract with Kanopy.[75] Not only was this a considerable circumvention of library staff, but according to Katelyn, from her understanding of the contract signed with the library, "Kanopy should not have retained this patron information for any reason. Kanopy should not have accessed those email addresses after the library's contract ended."[76] Katelyn was not the only one to relay this story in an interview—indeed Sarah mentioned it as well in their interview. The extent to which other similarly situated platforms are keeping and potentially exploiting patron data against the library's interests is unknown.

More research and analysis of OverDrive, Kanopy, and other platforms is needed to investigate the nature of their role, how they use their power, and the influence they may or may not have in this space. While libraries rely on these platforms to lend digital content to their patrons, they are at significant risk of exploitation in these relationships and under this new property regime.

Librarians as Advocates for Change

Librarians are exerting their right not to be excluded from the digital content market for the good of their members, communities, and institutions. They are engaging with a property regime that thinks of ebooks simply as the property of the private owner to exclude, but are asserting their right to 'not be excluded.'[77] Librarians are not neutral actors simply standing by and watching this property regime change happen. They resist these changes and advocate for their right to own and lend digital books, just like physical books, through legal avenues, digital campaigns, and developing their own platforms.

---

75 Katelyn, discussion.

76 Katelyn, discussion.

77 Maharawal et al., *Contested*.

All participants interviewed for this research shared similar concerns. However, they engaged with the issue in distinct ways. The New York University (NYU)-based eBook Study Group advocates for fair ebook pricing through the United States state-level courts.[78] They see legal cases as the way forward in their fight for fair ebook prices.[79] Juliya Ziskina, a Policy Fellow at eBook Study Group, highlights the reasons legal fights are essential, based on this new digital property regime being faced by libraries and privacy issues inherent in using digital lending platforms:

> [Ebooks] sit on a third-party aggregator, like OverDrive, which is a huge business. They collect all sorts of information. And there really aren't limits on it, which is horrifying. Libraries have been such important stewards of privacy and confidentiality, and all of a sudden, we're shifting away to ebooks and to reading digital books. And we're saying that (privacy) doesn't matter anymore, or that it's different for an ebook somehow. Why? That shouldn't be the case. It's a weird situation with this middleman, OverDrive... So this legislation basically aims to make contracts between publishers and rights holders and libraries more fair. Because the strange situation for libraries has gotten so bad that they need help. This is a consumer protection issue. Libraries are participants in the market, they are consumers, and they fall under consumer protection, and procurement law. A state has the ability and the power legally to regulate contracts between all sorts of entities. Why can't contracts between libraries and publishers also be regulated, so that

---

78 "The Licensed Library Ebook Market Is Unsustainable.," eBook Study Group, accessed January 10, 2024, https://www.ebookstudygroup.org/the_problem.

79 "New State Bills Aim to Improve Access to Ebooks for Libraries.," eBook Study Group, accessed January 29, 2024, https://www.ebookstudygroup.org/solving_problem_state_by_state.

(publishers) can't charge insane prices, and can't prevent a library from making accessible copies or preserving?[80]

Many online campaigns to educate the public about the issues with library ebook lending have gained traction in the last five years. One international example is #ebookSOS, a social media campaign developed by three academic librarians in the United Kingdom in response to the frustrating unavailability, high prices, and restrictive licences of ebooks during the COVID-19 lockdowns.[81] In North America, the Canadian Urban Libraries Council used the hashtag #econtentforlibraries in 2019 to raise awareness about Canada's lack of access and high cost of ebooks and audiobooks.[82] In 2023, the Internet Archive, supported by many other US-based library organizations, launched Battle for Libraries, a petition supporting their ongoing court case, libraries' digital rights, and an open internet with safe, uncensored access to knowledge.[83]

Library Futures, another NYU-based group, is at the forefront of the fight for library rights, especially in the ebook market.[84] They have been prolific in supporting all libraries, launching campaigns, hosting webinars and conferences, and engaging with many partner organizations. Director Jennie Rose Halperin indicates that there are more fundamental issues underlying

---

80 Juliya Ziskina, ((Policy Fellow at eBook Study Group) in discussion with the author, November 2023.

81 "Campaign to Investigate the Library Ebook Market," Campaign to Investigate the Library ebook Market, accessed November 21, 2022, https://academicebookinvestigation.org/.

82 "Stronger #eContentForLibraries," Stronger #eContentForLibraries, accessed January 11, 2024, https://econtentforlibraries.org/.

83 "Battle for Libraries."

84 Jennie Rose Halperin, "Library Futures Releases 2022 Annual Report," June 5, 2023, https://libraryfutures.net/post/library-futures-releases-2022-annual-report.

her drive to do her work.[85] The issues she sees encompass more than just privacy and equality.[86] At stake in this new property regime is the rights of every library, librarian and their users:

> In an anti-ownership ebook economy, the big difference is that you now have an intermediary, a platform, whose primary incentive is to collect as much data from patrons and money from libraries as they possibly can. For example, Hoopla collects an enormous amount of data from patrons. In the advocacy campaign we worked on, Hoopla had no stated collection development policy and was circulating hate speech due to a coordinated, unmonitored campaign by bad faith actors, and there are a lot of things that bother me about that. What it says to me is that this company thinks that public library patrons, people who can't afford to buy books, don't deserve accurate, vetted information. I think it's really exploitative. They're treating libraries and librarians like they don't know how to do the job they were trained for. Like they don't deserve to do their own collection development, because they're underfunded. And then I hear OverDrive at conferences saying, "We want to be the Costco of libraries". Is that what you think we deserve? That the reading public deserves Costco? And Costco is great, but it is still a big box corporate store. I just think that the public deserves more than a cheap goods and surveillance model.[87]

Advocacy campaigns around privacy concerns inherent in online reading platforms are also building momentum and are increasingly important. OverDrive's power to operate across

---

85 Jennie Rose Halperin (Director of Library Futures) in discussion with the author, November 2023.

86 Halperin, discussion.

87 Halperin.

domains allows it to collect and control content and consumer data, facilitating surveillance of library patrons in this new digital property regime.[88] It is unclear whether platforms are using the data they collect on library patrons ethically,[89] because while libraries are unique institutions with robust and strict privacy standards for their patrons, ebooks and the data collected from use in North American libraries currently sit in a legal grey zone.[90]

While many groups are fighting for the larger control over the content they pay for and the rights of patrons, others are looking at ways to reshape the platform-library relationship and break up OverDrive's power as the most significant player in the market. Despite the issues with platforms as the go-to method of lending digital content, new entrants into the market present themselves as viable alternatives, though perhaps without addressing the underlying issues inherent in digital lending platforms. The Digital Public Library of America, using the New York Public Library's SimpleE software, has launched Palace Project, a nonprofit digital content platform which could redistribute some of the power and control held by platforms back to libraries. Indeed, many librarians interviewed in this research view the nonprofit more favourably than any of the other corporate platforms available to them. However, there are still some hurdles to be overcome before this platform becomes a real alternative. Despite Palace Project cutting what seems to be an exclusive and lucrative deal with Amazon to host some of its titles otherwise unavailable to other libraries, cost and content from the Big Five publishers are still issues. Michael, who offers the platform to his library members and supports the organization, thinks that the nonprofit status

---

88 Lamdan, *Data Cartels*.

89 Gross, "Surprisingly."

90 Lamdan, *Data Cartels*.

could give Palace a real competitive advantage over the other, corporate platforms.[91] However, there are still challenges:

> Right now, they're not able to offer the price breaks—although with magazines, they'd be charging as far less than OverDrive does—because they need enough libraries to participate, to have the money to make it sustainable. They can't keep running it on grants forever. If we could have enough libraries participate and there's no profit incentive, perhaps we could begin to see lower cost from a vendor rather than pumping money into, let's face it, a multimillion even billion-dollar enterprise like OverDrive.[92]

According to Michael, having people switch from OverDrive to Palace may be a challenge, as there's loyalty to OverDrive within the library community.[93] While librarians think of themselves as progressive and adopting new technologies, Michael's experience tells him that librarians are, in part, uncertain about switching platforms.[94] After putting considerable time and effort into learning one ebook lending system, Michael believes that many librarians and library systems are hesitant to adopt new practices and switch players, despite the potential benefits.[95] Some librarians he's worked with struggle with adopting new technology, whether that's due to time constraints from overloaded schedules, a preference for what is known over what is unknown, or low digital literacy and knowledge of how different technologies could benefit the libraries.[96]

---

91 Blackwell, discussion.

92 Blackwell.

93 Blackwell.

94 Blackwell.

95 Blackwell.

96 Blackwell.

Despite these challenges, library advocates continue to fight for a future with more content available for libraries. They are skeptical of consolidation in the publisher and platform market and some doubt whether legal battles for what they consider fair lending standards will be successful, despite positive public and private support from key players.

Conclusion

Despite the other significant challenges facing libraries, this issue is important as it can reshape how ownership of digital materials is understood across society. The current property regime governing libraries is changing towards one where libraries cannot preserve or share their materials. The issue of ebook licensing impacts society's right to information and privacy and the rights of libraries to own, lend, and preserve materials, their most basic civil functions. Libraries without materials to lend are not libraries; this change to one of North America's most important public institutions should worry anyone who cares about free speech, democracy, and civil life.

The words of the librarians featured here are just a snapshot of the interviews conducted as a part of this research; more data will be available in the author's thesis. However, the role of platforms as powerful but potentially untrustworthy actors in the space is clear. Digital material lending is only growing across libraries. Questions of digital property rights are only growing more critical as piracy and artificial intelligence demand more extensive and larger datasets for training their large language models.[97] Digital materials will only take up

---

[97] Dan Milmo, "Sarah Silverman Sues OpenAI and Meta Claiming AI Training Infringed Copyright," *The Guardian*, July 10, 2023, sec. Technology, https://www.theguardian.com/technology/2023/jul/10/Sarah-silverman-sues-openai-meta-copyright-infringement.

more of a library's collection in the future.[98] Libraries must find a solution to this unsustainable situation before platforms take over control of a library's entire collection. Our digital future is too important to be left unregulated and in the hands of monopoly-building corporations.

---

98 BookNet Canada, "Tapping Into Ebooks: Ebook Use in Canada," 2022.

Appendix A

Interview Questions—Topic Guide

Preamble

Before we get started, I'd like to take a moment to review the study's letter of information and consent with you.

- Did you have the chance to read it?
- Do you have any questions?
- Provided you have no [further] questions and consent to the interview being audio recorded, we can begin!

Biographical

- Can you tell me a about your background in this field?
- How did you become involved in this work?

Purposes

- How did your group come to be involved in the libraries? And the library ebook issue?
- What are your objectives in undertaking your work?

Making Sense of the Environment

- What challenges have you faced in doing your work?
- What obstacles have you encountered in your work?

Strategies and Tactics

- What strategies have you found the most useful in your work, and any other work related to libraries and/or ebooks you engage in?
- What tactics and techniques do you use to further your work?
- Have you ever experienced pushback, harassment, or intimidation in your work?

Going Forward

- What new moves do you see emerging in this field in the future?
- What is next in your work, personally and more generally?

Bibliography

ALA and Joint Digital Content Working Group. "The Need for Change: A Position Paper on E-Lending," December 2020. http://www.ala.org/tools/librariestransform/working-group-libraries-and-digital-content.

Albanese, Andrew. "OverDrive to Acquire Kanopy." *PublishersWeekly.Com*, June 9, 2021. https://www.publishersweekly.com/pw/by-topic/industry-news/libraries/article/86608-overdrive-to-acquire-kanopy.html.

Alvarez León, Luis F. "Property Regimes and the Commodification of Geographic Information: An Examination of Google Street View." *Big Data & Society* 3, no. 2 (December 1, 2016). https://doi.org/10.1177/2053951716637885.

Amyot, Maureen, Callan Bignoli, Jenn Bruneau, Clayton Cheever, Andrea Fiorillo, Jason Homer, Alison Macrina, Caitlin Staples, and Jennifer Wertkin. "Hoopla Has a Content Problem: Here's How To Fix It." *Library Journal*, August 23, 2022. https://www.libraryjournal.com/story/hoopla-has-a-content-problem-heres-how-to-fix-it-backtalk.

"Battle for Libraries." Accessed January 30, 2024. https://www.battleforlibraries.com/.

Blackwell, Michael. Interview with Michael Blackwell from St. Mary's County Library and Readers First, January 2024.

Blomley, Nicholas. "Foreword" In *Contested Property Claims: What Disagreement Tells Us About Ownership*, edited by Ownership Maja Hojer Bruun, Maja Hojer, Patrick J. L. Cockburn, Bjarke Skærlund Risager and Mikkel Thorup, xxi-xvi. New York: Routledge, 2019.

BookNet Canada. "Tapping Into Ebooks: Ebook Use in Canada," 2022.

Campaign to investigate the Library ebook market. "Campaign to Investigate the Library Ebook Market." Accessed November 21, 2022. https://academicebookinvestigation.org/.

Canadian Urban Institute Institut Urbain du Canada. "OVERDUE: The Case for Canada's Public Libraries," October 2023. https://canurb.org/publications/overdue/.

Canfield, Matthew. "Property Regimes." In *The Oxford Handbook of Law and Anthropology*, edited by Marie-Claire Foblets, Mark Goodale, Maria Sapignoli, and Olaf Zenker, 0. Oxford University Press, 2022. https://doi.org/10.1093/oxfordhb/9780198840534.013.23.

Courtney, Kyle K., and Juliya Ziskina. "The Publisher Playbook: A Brief History of the Publishing Industry's Obstruction of the Library Mission." Pre-print, 2023. https://dash.harvard.edu/handle/1/37374618.

De Castell, Christina, Joshua Dickison, Trish Mau, Mark Swartz, Robert Tiessen, Amanda Wakaruk, and Christina Winter. "Controlled Digital Lending of Library Books in Canada." *Partnership: The Canadian Journal of Library and Information Practice and Research* 17, no. 2 (December 21, 2022): 1–35. https://doi.org/10.21083/partnership.v17i2.7100.

eBook Study Group. "New State Bills Aim to Improve Access to Ebooks for Libraries." Accessed January 29, 2024. https://www.ebookstudygroup.org/solving_problem_state_by_state.

eBook Study Group. "The Licensed Library Ebook Market Is Unsustainable." Accessed January 10, 2024. https://www.ebookstudygroup.org/the_problem.

Freeman, Lisa M, and Nick Blomley. "Enacting Property: Making Space for the Public in the Municipal Library." *Environment and Planning C: Politics and Space* 37, no. 2 (March 1, 2019): 199–218. https://doi.org/10.1177/2399654418784024.

Giblin, Rebecca, and Cory Doctorow. *Chokepoint Capitalism: How to Beat Big Tech, Tame Big Content, and Get Artists Paid*. Boston: Beacon Press, 2022. (Overdrive).

Giblin, Rebecca, Jenny Kennedy, Kimberlee G. Weatherall, Daniel Ian Gilbert, Julian Thomas, and Francois Petitjean. "Available—But Not Accessible? Investigating Publisher E-Lending Licensing Practices." SSRN Scholarly Paper. Rochester, NY, October 4, 2018. https://papers.ssrn.com/abstract=3346199.

Gold, Debra. "Research Guides: Copyright Information & Resources: Fair Dealing & Flowchart." Accessed January 11, 2024. https://libguides.lakeheadu.ca/c.php?g=450304&p=3075879.

Gorman, Michael. *Our Enduring Values: Librarianship in the 21st Century*. Chicago: American Library Association, 2000.

Gross, Daniel A. "The Surprisingly Big Business of Library E-Books." *The New Yorker*, September 2, 2021. https://www.newyorker.com/news/annals-of-communications/an-app-called-libby-and-the-surprisingly-big-business-of-library-e-books.

Halperin, Jennie Rose. Director of Library Futures in discussion with the author, November 2023.

Halperin, Jennie Rose. "Library Futures Releases 2022 Annual Report," June 5, 2023. https://libraryfutures.net/post/library-futures-releases-2022-annual-report.

Hansen, David R., and Kyle K. Courtney. "A White Paper on Controlled Digital Lending of Library Books." Preprint. LawArXiv, September 24, 2018. https://doi.org/10.31228/osf.io/7fdyr.

Interview with a digital content expert, December 2023.

Johnson, Sarah. Sarah from Springfield Public Library, in discussion with author, November 2023.

Katelyn. Katelyn, in discussion with the author, December 2023.

Klinenberg, Eric. *Palaces for the People: How Social Infrastructure Can Help Fight Inequality, Polarization, and the Decline of Civic Life*. First edition. New York: Crown, 2018.

Knowledge Rights 21. "A Position Statement from Knowledge Rights 21 on eBooks and eLending," May 2022. https://www.knowledgerights21.org/wp-content/uploads/2022/10/eBookPositionPaper150522.pdf.

Lamdan, Sarah. Data Cartels: The Companies That Control and Monopolize Our Information. Stanford: Stanford University Press, 2022.

Lamdan, Sarah, Jason Schultz, Michael Weinberg, and Claire Woodcock. "The Anti-Ownership Ebook Economy: How Publishers and Platforms Have Reshaped the Way We Read in the Digital Age." *SSRN Electronic Journal*, 2023. https://doi.org/10.2139/ssrn.4511975.

Library Freedom Project. "We Demand Accountability from Hoopla Digital and OverDrive Regarding the Platforming of Fascist…." *Medium* (blog), March 3, 2022. https://libraryfreedom.medium.com/we-demand-accountability-from-hoopla-digital-and-over-drive-regarding-the-platforming-of-fascist-c47c88e62ddc.

Maharawal, Manissa, Shiri Pasternak, Nick Blomley, Miguel A. Martínez López, Maja Hojer Bruun, Mike Fabris (Krebs), Maria Persdotter, Erin M. B. McElroy, and Bjarke Skærlund Risager. *Contested Property Claims: What Disagreement Tells Us About Ownership*. Routledge, 2018. Academia.edu

May, Micah. "A Conversation with Michael Blackwell on Maximizing Ebooks Access." *Digital Public Library of America* (blog), January 11, 2021. https://dp.la/news/qa-with-michael-blackwell-director-st-marys-county-library-maryland.

Milliot, Jim. "Over the Past 25 Years, the Big Publishers Got Bigger—and Fewer." PublishersWeekly.com. Accessed July 27, 2023. https://www.publishersweekly.com/pw/by-topic/industry-news/publisher-news/article/89038-over-the-past-25-years-the-big-publishers-got-bigger-and-fewer.html.

Milmo, Dan. "Sarah Silverman Sues OpenAI and Meta Claiming AI Training Infringed Copyright." *The Guardian*, July 10, 2023, sec. Technology. https://www.theguardian.com/technology/2023/jul/10/Sarah-silverman-sues-openai-meta-copyright-infringement.

Nawotka, Ed. "Digital Book World: Startups Are Entering 'A New Age.'" PublishersWeekly.com, January 18, 2023. https://www.publishersweekly.com/pw/by-topic/digital/retailing/article/91317-digital-book-world-startups-are-entering-a-new-age.html.

Nielsen, Rasmus Kleis, and Sarah Anne Ganter. *The Power of Platforms: Shaping Media and Society*. Oxford Studies in Digital Politics. New York, NY: Oxford University Press, 2022.

Parker, Carmi. Carmi Parker from Whatcom County Library System in discussion with the authorNovember 2023.

Perzanowski, Aaron, and Jason Schultz. *The End of Ownership: Personal Property in the Digital Economy*, 2016. https://doi.org/10.7551/mitpress/10524.001.0001.

Potash, Steve. "Thoughts from a Digital Advocate: Pursuing the Holy Grail of Library eBook Models." *OverDrive Steve* (blog), February 22, 2021. https://overdrivesteve.com/pursuing-the-holy-grail-of-library-ebook-models/.

Rachel, Noorda, and Inman Berens Kathi. "Digital Public Library Ecosystem 2023." ALA, 2023.

Riegelhaupt, Kathleen. Kathleen Riegelhaupt, the Director of eReading at The New York Public Library, in discussion with the author, November 2023.

Rowan, Elena. "Requesting Article," August 15, 2023.

Soler, Rafa. "Library Associations across Europe Joint Call for Action on eBooks." *Knowledge Rights 21* (blog), April 24, 2023. https://www.knowledgerights21.org/news-story/library-associations-across-europe-joint-call-for-action-on-ebooks/.

Srnicek, Nick. *Platform Capitalism*. 1 online resource (vi, 171 pages) vols. Theory Redux. Cambridge, UK ; Polity Press, 2017. EBSCOhost.

Stone, Brad. "Amazon Erases Orwell Books From Kindle." *The New York Times*, July 18, 2009, sec. Technology. https://www.nytimes.com/2009/07/18/technology/companies/18amazon.html.

Stronger #eContentForLibraries. "Stronger #eContentForLibraries." Accessed January 11, 2024. https://econtentforlibraries.org/.

Whitney, Paul, and Christina de Castell. "Trade eBooks in Libraries—The Changing Landscape," December 16, 2016. https://repository.ifla.org/handle/123456789/2028.

Wolf, Christine. "The Big Five Publishers: Who Are They?" Substack newsletter. *Writers' Haven by Christine Wolf* (blog), February 11, 2024. https://christinewolf.substack.com/p/the-big-five-publishers-who-are-they.

Ziskina, Juliya. Juliya Ziskina, a Policy Fellow at eBook Study Group, in discussion with the author, November 2023.

Entanglements
How Academic and Commercial Streaming Film Platforms are Reshaping Academic Libraries, Research, and Learning

lisa Hooper

The value of film as a pedagogical tool in higher education has grown exponentially in recent years. Libraries are pivoting to meet surging demand for films to use as teaching and learning resources in higher education as well as meet end-user expectations that film will be delivered streaming rather than via physical discs. As academic film distributors shifted from physical disc vending to streaming delivery platforms, the previously straightforward task of purchasing DVDs or Blu-rays became a much more complex exercise that required navigating licensing rights, vendor-designed purchasing models, discoverability, accessibility, and significantly higher costs. Collection development for film continues to grow increasingly complex as companies providing streaming video on demand (SVOD) exert power and control over access, creative practices, distribution and collection practices, the market, and users.

Themes from Rasmus Kleis Nielsen and Sarah Anne Ganter's book *The Power of Platforms: Shaping Media and Society* will surface throughout this chapter's examination of how SVOD platforms apply power and control at all levels, from the creative process to distribution to consumption.[1] This chapter will also explore how market dominance and supply-side scale endow a few platforms with the capacity to develop field-changing technical protocols and reset standards of practice across industries (filmmaking, distribution, marketing, librarianship, and education). Finally, the chapter will delve into how platform-based practices in information asymmetry lead to data determinism, impacting what we see and when we see it on a platform. Entangled, in a sense, in a web of demand, customer captivity, standard revisions, and data asymmetry, libraries are increasingly diminished in their capacity to provide access and preserve the filmic cultural record, while SVODs, especially commercial platforms, are repositioning to become both providers and keepers of cultural heritage.

Understanding Demand for Streaming in Academic Libraries

Streaming film use on academic campuses has experienced explosive growth over the past 11 years. Researchers at the University of South Carolina reported a pre-pandemic increase of 236% in streaming film use from fiscal year 2016/17 to fiscal year 2019/20.[2] Similarly, researchers at the University of San Diego noted demand for streaming film tripled during the pandemic and remained strong even after the university returned to in-person instruction following the initial phase of

---

1   Rasmus Kleis Nielsen and Sarah Anne Ganter, *The Power of Platforms: Shaping Media and Society* (New York: Oxford University Press, 2022).

2   Christian Lear, "Controlled Digital Lending of Video Resources: Ensuring the Provision of Streaming Access to Videos for Pedagogical Purposes in Academic Libraries," *Journal of Copyright in Education and Librarianship* 5, no. 1 (2022): 3.

the COVID-19 pandemic.[3] This massive increase in demand for streaming content at a single institution is equally borne out by national studies assessing the adoption of streaming film in academic libraries. An early study in 2010 showed that only 33% of academic institutions were offering streaming video options to their users.[4] Just three years later, another study revealed that 70% of academic libraries were providing streaming.[5] By 2015, that percentage rose to 84.5%[6] and continued to increase to 96.7% adoption by spring 2021.[7]

One of the major drivers for increased adoption is changing pedagogical practices in higher education, with an increased perception of film as an impactful teaching tool. A 2023 Ithaka S+R report found that faculty across the disciplines are now using film, with different survey participants describing film as a "tool for illustrating and reinforcing class concepts,"[8] to "engage different learning styles by diversifying learning modalities,"[9] to create an access point to "voices and experienc-

---

3   Millicent Fullmer, "Future Proofing Streaming Video Acquisitions: A Medium Sized Academic Library Adapts," *Technical Services Quarterly* 40, no. 2 (2023): 61, 68. https://doi.org/10.1080/07317131.2023.2187109.

4   Primary Research Group, Survey of Academic Libraries quoted in deg farrelly and Jane Hutchison, "ATG Special Report: Academic Library Streaming Video: Key Findings from the National Survey," in *Against the Grain* (2014) 26/5, p. 73.

5   deg farrelly and Jane Hutchison, "ATG Special Report: Academic Library Streaming Video: Key Findings from the National Survey," *Against the Grain* 26, no. 5 (2014): 73.

6   deg farrelly and Jane Hutchison Surdi, "Academic Library Streaming Video Revisited" (presentation, American Library Association Annual Conference, Orlando, FL, June 26, 2016). Accessed December 28, 2023 https://keep.lib.asu.edu/items/357.

7   Gisèle Tanasse, "Implementing and Managing Streaming Media Services in Academic Libraries" (Chicago: ACRL/Choice, 2021), 9. http://choice360.org/librarianship/whitepaper.

8   Ruby MacDougall and Dylan Ruediger, *Teaching with Streaming Video: Understanding Instructional Practices, Challenges, and Support Needs* (New York, NY: Ithaka S+R, 2023), 7. https://doi.org/10.18665/sr.318216.

9   MacDougall and Ruediger, *Teaching*, 8.

es" that might not be reflected in classroom demographics,[1] and to enhance cultural and linguistic understanding.[2] While faculty in cinema and language studies remain some of the most frequent users, a comprehensive survey found that faculty "across disciplines have incorporated more streaming video into their teaching since the start of the pandemic."[3] Faculty in the arts and humanities were especially likely to utilize library-provided streaming film resources.[4]

Customer Captivity, Scale, and Market Dominance

The sheer quantity of commercial and academic SVODs create an illusion of abundance and access to meet demand. But this is more perception, less reality. Academic streaming platforms have created exclusive or near-exclusive distribution agreements that, on the one hand, save libraries from paying twice for the same title(s) as is often the case with overlap in journal subscription packages. On the other hand, this practice leaves libraries entirely reliant on multiple SVOD platforms for access to their exclusive content. For example, librarians looking to provide access to films produced by 20th Century Fox can only license these films from Criterion Pictures USA, films from Criterion Pictures can only be licensed from Kanopy, films from Ro*Co can only be licensed from Alexander Street Press, films from Bullfrog Films can only be licensed from Docuseek2, and so on. In this current distribution model, libraries *must* do business with multiple platforms if they are to fulfill their core standards of practice to "provide access to collections sufficient in quality, depth, diversity, format, and

---

1 MacDougall and Ruediger, 10.
2 MacDougall and Ruediger, 11.
3 MacDougall and Ruediger, 6.
4 MacDougall and Ruediger, 6.

currency to support the research and teaching missions of the institution."[5] To provide access to course-required content, libraries have no choice but to find a way to fund and manage licensing (both subscription and title-by-title) from multiple academic streaming platforms at significantly higher per title costs.[6] A 2021 survey of North American academic institutions found that many libraries are now doing just that, with 94% of responding libraries licensing individual titles and 90% maintaining active subscriptions.[7]

Media librarians recognize that faculty want more than what is available through academic streaming platforms. Indeed, many faculty often request titles exclusive to commercial streaming platforms including Netflix, Amazon Prime Video, Disney+, HBO, Hulu, and Criterion, among others.[8] Many faculty, especially in cinema and media studies, "require up-to-date streaming content beyond that which is available on YouTube or Kanopy and have little choice but to use direct to

---

5   American Library Association. "5. Collections," *Standards for Libraries in Higher Education*, 2018. Accessed January 14, 2024. https://www.ala.org/acrl/standards/standardslibraries.

6   For example of significant cost increases created by the shift from physical formats to streaming, *The Grand Hotel Budapest*, release to DVD and Blu-ray in June 2014, could have been purchased on Blu-ray for $19.96 through Amazon https://web.archive.org/web/20140626022639/http://www.amazon.com/movies-tv-dvd-bluray/b?ie=UTF8&node=2625373011.) Ten years later, this film is available today for libraries to license through Criterion Pictures on demand at a cost of $100 per year (note, pricing is not posted to this vendor's website. Pricing described here is the annual licensing cost at this author's institution). Criterion Collection's *A Hard Day's Night* could have been purchased on Blu-ray in 2014 for $24.99 (https://web.archive.org/web/20140708042258/http://www.amazon.com/movies-tv-dvd-bluray/b?ie=UTF8&node=2625373011) while librarians today can only license streaming access from Kanopy at a cost of $150 for 1 year of access or $350 for 3 years of access.

7   Danielle M. Cooper, Dylan Ruediger, Makala Skinner. *Streaming Media Licensing and Purchasing Practices at Academic Libraries: Survey Results*. (Chicago, IL: Ithaka S+R, 2022), 5.

8   See Helen N. Levenson and Shawn V. Lombardo. "The State of Streaming Video Content at Academic Libraires," *Collection Management*, 48, no. 4 (2023): p. 397-408, https://doi.org/10.1080/01462679.2023.2255561; Lear, 7; and Tanasse, 5.

consumer subscription services."[9] Achieving this, especially in the fields of cinema and media studies, is no small matter. As Carley Lamphere observed, "no single platform can meet every need of a user, which means users often have to maintain multiple subscriptions."[10] Consumers, and now academics, are at the mercy of studio and platform owners, who "have thrown users into the middle of their content wars"[11] while also locking content behind restrictive individual user agreements that explicitly limit use to noncommercial private settings.[12] This is significant in a cultural moment when faculty are increasingly seeking to lower economic barriers to academic success by incorporating learning materials that are open access, provided at no cost to students by the library, or are otherwise comparatively low-cost course material for students.[13] No longer able to fully rely on their institutional library to provide access to course-required material, faculty requiring films on these commercial platforms are held captive by the exclusive distribution policies and limiting end-user agreements ubiquitous to commercial streaming platforms. These business practices are now deeply impacting student learning and leave faculty with only bad choices: they can abide the terms of use and not include contemporary and culturally significant content in their courses; they can violate their terms of use and include this content in their courses; or they can require their students

---

9   MacDougall and Ruediger, *Teaching*, 16.

10 Carley Lamphere, "Streaming Media: An Access and Preservation Game Changer" in *Online Searcher* (May/June 2020) 44/3, 31.

11 Lamphere, "Streaming Media," 33.

12 See Netflix, Inc, Netflix Terms of Use, January 24, 2024, https://help.netflix.com/legal/termsofuse; Amazon Prime Video Terms of Use, https://www.primevideo.com/help?nodeId=202095490; Disney Terms of Use, https://disneytermsofuse.com/english/.

13 Chana Joffe-Walt and Ira Glass, "550: 3 Miles," March 13, 2015, in *This American Life*, produced by WBEZ, podcast, MP3 audio, https://www.thisamericanlife.org/550/three-miles.

to create personal subscription accounts and increase out of pocket learning costs for their students. This condition of customer captivity is just one element of a larger relationship redefining access, preservation, research, learning, and the long cultural record.

There is a mutually reinforcing relationship between customer captivity, market dominance, and supply-side scale. Some academic platform representatives describe a sense of vendor oversaturation[14] when in fact the field is experiencing clear market dominance created and maintained by customer captivity and supply-side scale. This becomes evident in academia when looking at platform adoption across academic institutions. Kanopy (Overdrive), Alexander Street Press (ProQuest/Clarivate), Films on Demand/Films Media Group, Swank Digital Campus, and Naxos are the top five most used academic platforms in the United States according to the 2021 survey.[15] However, among these top five service providers, adoption strongly favors just two, with Alexander Street Press and Kanopy being used in 80% and 85% of libraries surveyed, respectively. Films on Demand/Films Media Group has been adopted by 68% of libraries and Swank by 66%, and the fifth, Naxos, in just 51% of libraries.[16] These heavily-utilized academic platforms, then, not only have customer captivity but they also have the most financial resources to effectively manage supply-side scale. For both commercial and academic SVOD platforms, supply-side scale looks like an "ability to spread the fixed costs of content, marketing, and technology across a subscriber base

---

14 Private informal conversation between this author and various platform representatives.

15 Cooper et al., *Streaming*, 6.

16 Cooper et al., 6.

vastly larger than any other competitor's."[17] As Jonathan Knee observed in *Platform Delusion: Who Wins and Who Loses in the Age of Tech Titans*, "the most prevalent sources of industrial strength have been in the mutually reinforcing competitive advantages of supply-side scale and customer captivity."[18] As libraries divert more of their limited financial resources to a small number of academic platforms, they have less money to spend on emerging and subject-specific platforms. The platforms with high subscription rates have more financial resources to manage their fixed costs and continue growing the platform. Meanwhile, platforms with lower subscription rates, especially niche subject specialists and emerging platforms, have far fewer financial resources to manage their fixed costs. As larger platforms continue to grow and develop their product they become increasingly attractive to cash-strapped libraries, while smaller platforms may not have the resources to develop competitively.

The impacts on library collections can be profound when we look at the content that emerging academic streaming platforms are offering. In 2021, Grasshopper Films launched Projectr to offer academic streaming access to international independent cinema. Kweli.tv, the only platform to date offering US academic institutions access to film and television from Africa and the African diaspora, entered the academic market in 2022. Pragda launched PragdaStream in 2023 to offer streaming access to film from Latin America, South America, Spain, and other Spanish-speaking communities. In each of these cases, their content is available near exclusively or exclusively

---

17 Jonathan Knee, *The Platform Delusion: Who Wins and Who Loses in the Age of Tech Titans* (New York: Penguin Press, 2021), 137.

18 Knee, *The Platform Delusion*, 135.

on their platforms.[19] Certainly, plenty of content about the global south and about non-western European countries can be found on all the major platforms. However, content explicitly *from* these areas is far more prevalent on these newer platforms that hold a much smaller slice of the academic library market and, thus, have far less access to resources to maintain and grow their infrastructure.

Market dominance by the top five platforms, and the massive amount of funding it requires for libraries to maintain these subscriptions, make it incredibly difficult for emerging and independent platforms to enjoy wide adoption. For many institutions, the excessive costs of multiple subscriptions leave little to no financial resources left for new platform subscriptions. The only alternative—canceling a subscription to Kanopy, Alexander Street Press, or one of the other widely-used services—is a nonstarter given the high pedagogical value of the films these platforms exclusively offer. In other words, academic institutions are captive customers to the top five academic streaming platforms in the same way that cinema studies faculty are captive to Netflix or Amazon Prime Video.

The same is true in the commercial market with Netflix, Disney+, and Amazon dominating a robust field of streaming video services. Members of the filmmaking industry have found commercial practices so alarming that the Writers Guild of America (WGA) published a report calling for action to limit the market power these three companies are wielding:

> Deregulation and mergers have laid the groundwork for a future of increased market power that could soon leave just

---

19 At the time of writing, Kweli.tv was fully exclusive content while Grasshopper and Pragda continued to provide access to selections of their catalog on other major academic platforms. It is unclear if continued presence on Alexander Street Press and Kanopy is due to still active distribution agreements created prior to the launch of their platforms or if this is a failsafe to ensure some level of access for libraries unable to subscribe to their new platforms.

> three companies controlling what content is made, what consumers can watch, and how they can watch it. Disney, Amazon, and Netflix are positioning themselves to be the new gatekeepers of media, growing through acquisitions and using their increased power to disadvantage competitors, raise prices for consumers, and to push down wages for creative workers.... Without intervention, these conglomerates will seize control of the media landscape and the streaming era's advances for creativity and choice will be lost.[20]

While the WGA is looking ahead to the near future, companies like Netflix, Amazon Prime Video, and Disney+ already enjoy market dominance. By fall 2020, Netflix amassed 201 million subscribers, far surpassing its closest competitor, Amazon Prime Video, which was nearing 117 million subscribers by that same date. Disney+ held a distant third with 82 million subscribers. No other streaming platform came close to touching these top three.[21]

This trifecta of market dominance, scale, and customer captivity across both academic and commercial streaming platforms allows these platforms to flex an extraordinary level of power over the careers of faculty and students as the content they choose to make available, and not make available, shapes the research faculty are empowered to engage in and the learning and research experiences they design for their students.

---

20 Writers Guild of America, *The New Gatekeepers: How Disney, Amazon, and Netflix will Take Over Media* (Los Angeles, CA: Writers Guild of America, 2023). Accessed December 2023, https://www.wga.org/uploadedfiles/news_and_events/public_policy/GatekeepersReport23.pdf.

21 Julia Stoll, "Estimated Number of SVOD Subscribers Worldwide from 2020 to 2029, by Service," *Statista*, December 21, 2023. Accessed January 30, 2024, https://www.statista.com/statistics/1052770/global-svod-subscriber-count-by-platform/.

Re-Setting Standards

As they emerged in the industry, academic SVOD platforms developed distribution models that necessitated a radical shift in library practices. Physical media allowed libraries to purchase films and provide their students, faculty, and staff access to individual titles until the item wore out. This allowed libraries to collect for contemporary needs while also creating a cumulative record for future researchers. Academic SVOD platforms, however, have made buy-to-own obsolete or realistically far more fiscally difficult to attain. Academic platforms and rights holders often negotiate limited distribution terms, meaning most films are only available to academic libraries with short-term access licenses, typically only one or three years. While a growing number of titles are becoming available with long-term access options (e.g., digital site licenses and life-of-file), the average $500+ per title price-point is a significant financial barrier for many libraries. These limitations at the heart of streaming film distribution have forced a radical shift in how libraries perceive film collections. For many years, the growing prevalence of leasing and diminishing opportunity to own was perceived as an existential threat to academic library film collections[22] but is now so normal that this concern no longer figures in the literature. In other words, it is generally accepted that the majority of many libraries' digital film collections are now leased (often for short term access) rather than fully owned in perpetuity.

---

22 See John Vallier, "Twenty-First Century Academic Media Center: Killer App or Chindogu?" *Library Trends* 58, no. 3 (Winter 2010); Gary Handman, "License to Look: Evolving Models for Library Video Acquisition and Access," *Library Trends* 50, no. 3 (Winter 2010); Rachel King "House of Cards: The Academic Library Media Center in the Era of Streaming Video," *The Serials Librarian* (2014) 67:3, 289-306; Carly Lamphere, "Streaming Media: An Access and Preservation Game Changer" in *Internet Express* (May/June 2020), 44/3: 31-34.

Many academic SVODs also developed subscription packages as alternative licensing options. These models offer significant long-term cost savings for institutions that can afford the hefty up-front price tag, and they also provide access to extensive film collections. There is, however, a hidden trade-off when libraries sign on to these packaged compilations of films created by platforms far removed from the local institution. While the librarian is still important to selecting which subscriptions to maintain and serves as point of contact with end users, these subscription packages effectively circumvent a librarian's collection development expertise and knowledge of their institution's uniquely local needs in terms of collection gaps, faculty research and teaching needs, and student learning needs.

Several academic SVOD platforms have created a third purchasing model that attempts to place some collection building power back in the hands of librarians. These models include patron-driven acquisitions (PDA) and evidence-based acquisition (EBA) models. While some institutions have been able to make PDA work, many find the costs entirely unsustainable.[23] Evidence-based models usually require an upfront sum of money, often tens of thousands of dollars, to gain access to a platform's collections. This cost, even when split across multiple fiscal years, can be prohibitive for many libraries, and can either prevent them from adopting this model altogether or can require them to select one platform over another (a problem when so many films are exclusive to different platforms). In EBA models, platforms make their entire collection

---

[23] See Helen N. Levenson and Shawn V. Lombardo, "The State of Streaming Video Content at Academic Libraries," *Collection Management* 48, no. 4 (2023): 397-408; Sandra Gall Urban, "Evaluating Kanopy Access Models in *Academic Libraries: Balancing Demand and Budget Constraints, Collection Development*, 47, no. 1 (2022): 37-48; Elsa Loftis and Carly Lamphere, "Swimming Upstream in the Academic Library: Exploring Faculty Needs for Library Streaming Media Collections," *Evidence Based Library and Information Practice*, 18, no. 4 (2023): 68-83.

available for a predetermined length of time. At the end of the full access period, libraries can select a predetermined number of titles which they are able to retain with perpetual access, while the rest of the content on that platform gets locked down and access is removed. To obtain access to titles newly released to the platform, libraries will either resort to resource-consuming title-by-title short-term licensing or renewing costly EBA agreements to continue providing uninterrupted full access for their campus community.

Over the past 10 or so years, academic SVODs have easily shifted library values. Where libraries used to give preference to ownership, short-term licenses are now an accepted norm; where collection development once valued a focus on known and anticipated local needs, collection development now in part consists of choosing which standardized, industry-defined collection should be prioritized and which should be deprioritized; where collections could be built for long term access with one eye toward preservation, collections are now built with the short term in mind. Numerous informal conversations with vendor representatives and leaders over the years lead this author to believe that this shift of power away from libraries and to academic streaming platforms was not intentional. Indeed, conversations with sales representatives and industry leaders repeatedly reveal an enthusiasm and desire to provide the best content to as many people as possible. This power imbalance might simply be the "cost of doing business" in the transition from DVD supplier to streaming delivery platform, but it nonetheless creates unsettling ripples across academia of haves versus have-nots, of thrivers versus strivers.

Not to be outdone by academic platforms that are revolutionizing the business of film librarianship, consumer-direct SVODs also have extraordinary capacity to significantly alter technical standards and protocols that have a similarly profound impact on access. For example, Netflix holds the patent to an algorithm that selects, orders, and groups titles in recommendation lists personalized to the user based on user-supplied data. Another Netflix patent, WO2012138667, seeks to identify a user's mood based on user-supplied data and adjust customized recommendations accordingly.[24] As an early entry to commercial SVODs, Netflix became a leader in designing and implementing these user-focused algorithms that are now ubiquitous across all commercial streaming platforms. With these algorithms, user choice becomes more a matter of perceived choice, while the platforms use their power to design those choices. This heavy reliance on data and algorithms, as will be seen, are key to building and maintaining power among consumer-direct SVODs.

Algorithms, Data-Determinism, and Access

Unlike academic SVOD platforms which capture minimal individual user data,[25] commercial SVODs thrive on user data in a way that determines *who* watches *what*. User data drives decisions about what content to produce, and (thanks to those algorithmic patents) determines when to surface content on a platform and who gets to see it. This is, in effect, an exertion of power and control by commercial platforms over cultural creation, consumption, access, and preservation at levels unimaginable just a decade ago. As Sarah Arnold observed, "the Netflix user becomes classified as a set of data and the information drawn from this data becomes the primary form

---

24 Parminder Lally, "From Snail Mail to Streaming: The Netflix Intellectual Property Story," *Mondaq Business Summary* (12 March 2021).

25 Informal conversation between this author and academic streaming platform representative. Personal accounts on academic platforms enable users to create playlists and clips, but do not offer recommendations based on personal data-informed algorithms.

of knowledge produced by Netflix."[26] This data—every click, every trailer viewed, every second watched, every recommendation, etc.—is "fed back into the company's strategic decisions about original programming, licensing, and marketing."[27] The data collected and how it is used is obscure, at best, for the typical user, leading to extreme information asymmetry or an environment where the user has limited information about the platform and the platform has massive amounts of data about the user.[28] The consequences of this opaque algorithmic data determinism are far reaching.

One often discussed consequence of data determinism is the loss of a beloved title from a streaming platform catalog. In 2016, Marc Devoise, executive vice president and general manager of CBS Digital Media and CBS Interactive broke it down this way:

> We want to own as many past episodes as we can, but our consumption patterns show that viewers mostly watch current content… Some 60% of our viewership is current season on-demand, while 15% are watching streaming live TV; 25% of our traffic watches deep library content or past seasons.[29]

In other words, CBS (and others) sees lower profit gains with older and niche content, especially when licensing and residual costs associated with a title negatively impact a title's net

---

[26] Sarah Arnold, "Netflix and the Myth of Choice/Participation/Autonomy," in *The Netflix Effect: Technology and Entertainment in the 21st Century*, ed. Kevin McDonald and Daniel Smith-Rowsey (New York: Bloomsbury Publishing, 2016), 55.

[27] Ramon Lobato, *Netflix Nations: The Geography of Digital Distribution* (New York: New York University Press, 2019): 14.

[28] Nielsen and Ganter, *Power*, 21.

[29] Page Albiniak, "Why Your Show May be a Streaming No Show," *Broadcasting and Cable-Multichannel News* (April 18, 2016): 34.

revenue. The result is that titles producing insufficient revenue can remain locked within restrictive distribution agreements and, at best, get buried by the algorithms on the platform or, at worst, withdrawn from the public-facing catalog even while the platform still holds exclusive distribution rights. This practice prevents other distributors from acquiring the film or television series; the resulting low viewership and engagement makes it a less desirable title for commercial and academic vendors to pick up when it is finally released from the terms of the original distribution agreement. Such titles effectively vanish.

Commercial streaming platforms collect massive amounts of user data from wildly different communities, normalize it, and transform it into "recurring and therefore predictable patterns."[30] This data-determined algorithmic pattern not only generates recommendation lists, but also deeply influences *what* content is shown on the platform interface and to *whom*. As Neta Alexander observed, "the more information you (consciously or unconsciously) provide Netflix, the less likely you will encounter any 'great films' outside your comfort zone."[31] Alexander continued to make this important point: "the pursuit of the 'comfort zone' is based on the denial of the importance of contingency, serendipity, and potentiality within the formation of taste."[32] A closed feedback loop is created by this algorithm, defining and increasingly confining what the platform surfaces for each viewer. At the same time, the physical library collection's ability to keep pace and challenge the commercial platforms is increasingly diminished. In other words,

---

30 Neta Alexander, "Catered to Your Future Self: Netflix's Predictive Personalization and the Mathematization of Taste," in *The Netflix Effect: Technology and Entertainment in the 21st Century*, ed. Kevin McDonald and Daniel Smith-Rowsey (New York: Bloomsbury Publishing, 2016): 89.

31 Alexander, "Catered," 89.

32 Alexander, 90.

in the absence of a grounding counterbalance, data determinism baked into commercial streaming platforms places them in a position to direct (or even design) cultural consumption and access to creative cultural works.

Algorithms, Data Determinism, and Creative Cultural Outputs

Commercial SVOD platforms take their power over cultural production and consumption even further by deeply influencing *how* we watch. Leaning into the technologically-enabled binge-watching phenomenon, commercial SVODs "lead producers to tailor their programs for binge-watching, or at least incentivize a structural redesign of episodic narrative."[33] Netflix's *House of Cards* was a front runner in designing serial productions for binge watching.[34] Indeed, by embracing growing trends in binge-watching data, the show's producer, Beau Willimon, made it very clear that binge-watching was the plan all along, declaring "our goal is to shut down a portion of America for a whole day."[35] Through its premiere production, Netflix intentionally sought to radically change behavior patterns of a large number of individuals.

This intentional shift in creative styles that lead subscribers to binge-watching also, of course, influenced narrative design for the first time in decades. This model rendered recaps and periodicity superfluous and they were dropped, as Casey

---

33 Gerald Sim, "Individual Disruptors and Economic Gamechangers: Netflix, New Media and Neoliberalism" in *The Netflix Effect: Technology and Entertainment in the 21st Century*, ed. Kevin McDonald and Daniel Smith-Rowsey (New York: Bloomsbury Publishing, 2016): 189.

34 Casey McCormick, "'Forward is the Battle Cry': Binge-Viewing Netflix's House of Cards," in *The Netflix Effect: Technology and Entertainment in the 21st Century*, ed. Kevin McDonald and Daniel Smith-Rowsey (New York: Bloomsbury Publishing, 2016): 101.

35 Brian Stelter, "New Way to Deliver a Drama: All 13 Episodes in One Sitting," *The New York Times* (1923-) (Feb 1, 2013): A1.

McCormick observed, in favor of structures "that privilege user/text relationships over advertising mandates and monolithic, unidirectional structures of programming flow."[36] For viewers, this is not necessarily a bad thing, as it has the capacity to elevate the viewer's sense of emotional intensity and story immersion.[37] What is remarkable in this, however, is the power flex this was on the part of Netflix to significantly alter long-established narrative practices, to lead large numbers of individuals to change their habits, and to force major companies across several industries to develop entirely new marketing plans to fit this new viewing experience. In other words, Netflix wielded its power "to make and break connections,"[38] significantly altering sociocultural viewing practices as well as entrenched professional and business practices. There is no impermeable line for creators or consumers between content accessed through commercial or academic sources; these platform-driven changes in creative practices and consumer behavior ripple into academic sources as well.

Long-Term Access and Preservation

The current streaming platform environment casts doubt on the ability for libraries to secure access to creative cultural heritage content and to preserve it for continued access well into the future. As the American Library Association emphasizes, "we have a special obligation to ensure the free flow of information and ideas to present and future generations."[39] Through the unique process of licensing and distribution

---

36 McCormick, "Forward," 102.

37 McCormick, 101.

38 Neilsen and Ganter, *Power*, 21.

39 American Library Association, ALA Policy Manual, B.1.2 Code of Professional Ethics for Librarians, accessed January 27, 2024, https://www.ala.org/aboutala/governance/policymanual/updatedpolicymanual/section2/40corevalues.

agreements between vendors and rights holders for films, distributors can rarely truly sell a film to libraries. Instead, they offer access licenses, the longest-term being life-of-file. As any film librarian knows, these are the least common and the most expensive and still don't permit basic archiving activities; one-year and three-year access licenses are quite common. In the commercial realm, there is no guarantee of long-term access or preservation. In other words, neither academic nor commercial SVOD platforms enable meaningful long-term preservation practices by traditional institutional heritage keepers. SVOD platforms were originally designed as content delivery platforms. Academic platforms don't own the majority of their content, instead they distribute content with permission of the rights holder. Commercial platforms also began as sites of distribution, moving into production only relatively recently. They, too, have no legal capacity to engage in preservation measures for content they don't own, and they've demonstrated no interest in engaging in preservation practice for titles they do own. Whether rights holders recognize the long-term value of their film as a piece of the larger sociocultural record is debatable, as is whether they have the knowledge, technology, and funds required to engage in meaningful digital preservation practices.

Will film titles fall out of academic library collections as licenses and distribution rights expire? Will they be forgotten and left out of the historical record as sources of information and insights into past cultures? Current distribution methods indicate that this is a very real possibility. The power to make curatorial decisions for our future now rests, in many cases, in the hands of streaming film platforms and individual filmmakers. Academic librarians are keenly aware of how bias influences curatorial decisions and have made significant strides to remediate past oversights and monitor and adjust for emergent biases in our collections; the same is not necessarily true for

SVODs with no obligation to the future. This should be of critical concern to cultural historians and the LIS community who need to be in the vanguard pushing for increased transparency, acknowledgement of responsibility, and actionable commitments to cultural historical preservation and access.

Conclusion

Fundamental changes to the film distribution industry wrought by the streaming environment will continue to profoundly impact academic libraries. Streaming distribution models developed within the vast silo of the industry have turned traditional collection development practices for libraries on their head, with the effect of deeply disrupting and complicating our ability to collect with intention and attention to deeply local needs. Programs for preservation and long-term access have similarly been rendered impotent in face of these same policies and dollar-first industry values. Instead, this platform-woven web of customer captivity, market dominance, scale, technological dominance, and, in the case of commercial platforms, data-determinism, has fully entangled libraries in strategizing, prioritizing, planning, and endless licensing to a degree of complexity that didn't exist before streaming overtook the DVD. In the course of simply doing business, academic and commercial SVOD platforms have effectively circumscribed the academic library and repositioned themselves as both providers and keepers of filmic cultural memory.

Located far from a seemingly inaccessible seat of power, individual libraries appear to have few avenues available to reclaim some of this power. Organizations like the Film and Media Round Table[40] of the American Library Association and

---

40 https://www.ala.org/fmrt.

Video Trust,[41] however, might the last key. Their ongoing work to maintain positive relationships with vendors and film platforms has held the door open just a crack to opportunities for collectively advocating for more financially achievable distribution models as well as improvements to equitable long-term access and preservation. Much of their work, especially the annual Video Trust conference, creates opportunities for information and needs sharing as well as much-needed structured dialogue between librarians and film vendors and platforms. While both organizations have the potential to become impactful advocacy arms, the Film and Media Roundtable of the American Library Association is well-positioned to advocate for key educational and preservation rights with the United States Copyright Office. Video Trust, meanwhile, can further position itself to dialogue with current and aspiring independent filmmakers, working in partnership with related practitioners to develop information resources that will help independent filmmakers find ethically responsible distributors and expose them in an impactful way to the oft-overlooked educational market.

Bibliography

Albiniak, Page. "Why Your Show May be a Streaming No Show," *Broadcasting and Cable-Multichannel News*, 146, no. 15 (April 18, 2016), 34.

Alexander, Neta. "Catered to Your Future Self: Netflix's Predictive Personalization and the Mathematization of Taste." In *The Netflix Effect: Technology and Entertainment in the 21st Century*, edited by Kevin McDonald and Daniel Smith-Rowsey, 81-97. New York: Bloomsbury Publishing, 2016.

---

41 https://www.videotrust.org/.

American Library Association, ALA Policy Manual, B.1.2 Code of Professional Ethics for Librarians, accessed January 27, 2024, https://www.ala.org/aboutala/governance/policymanual/updatedpolicymanual/section2/40corevalues.

American Library Association. Standards for Libraries in Higher Education. Chicago, IL: American Libraries Association, 2018. Accessed January 14, 2024. https://www.ala.org/acrl/standards/standardslibraries.

Arnold, Sarah. "Netflix and the Myth of Choice/Participation/Autonomy." In *The Netflix Effect: Technology and Entertainment in the 21st Century*, edited by Kevin McDonald and Daniel Smith-Rowsey, 49-62. New York: Bloomsbury Publishing, 2016.

Cooper, Danielle M., Dylan Ruediger, and Makala Skinner. *Streaming Media Licensing and Purchasing Practices at Academic Libraries: Survey Results*. New York: Ithaka S+R, 2022.

Farrelly, deg and Jane Hutchison. "Academic Library Streaming Video: Key Findings from the National Survey." *Against the Grain* 26, no. 5 (2014): 73-75.

Farrelly, deg and Jane Hutchison Surdi. "Academic Library Streaming Video Revisited." Paper presented at the American Library Association Annual Conference, Orlando, FL, June 26, 2016. https://keep.lib.asu.edu/items/357.

Fullmer, Millicent. "Future Proofing Streaming Video Acquisitions: A Medium Sized Academic Library Adapts." *Technical Services Quarterly* 40, no. 2 (2023). https://doi.org/10.1080/07317131.2023.2187109.

Handman, Gary. "License to Look: Evolving Models for Library Video Acquisition and Access." *Library Trends*, 50, no. 3 (Winter 2010): 324-334.

Joffe-Walt, Chana and Ira Glass. "550: 3 Miles." produced by WBEZ. This American Life. March 13, 2015. Podcast, MP3 audio, https://www.thisamericanlife.org/550/three-miles.

King, Rachel. "House of Cards: The Academic Library Media Center in the Era of Streaming Video." *The Serials Librarian*, 64, no. 3 (2014): 389-306.

Knee, Jonathan. *The Platform Delusion: Who Wins and Who Loses in the Age of Tech Titans*. New York: Penguin Press, 2021.

Lally, Parminder. "From Snail Mail to Streaming: The Netflix Intellectual Property Story." *Mondaq Business Summary* (March 12, 2021).

Lamphere, Carley. "Streaming Media: An Access and Preservation Game Changer." *Online Searcher* 44, no. 3 (2020): 31-34.

Lear, Christian. "Controlled Digital Lending of Video Resources: Ensuring the Provision of Streaming Access to Videos for Pedagogical Purposes in Academic Libraries." *Journal of Copyright in Education and Librarianship*, 5, no. 1 (2022): 1-19.

Levenson, Helen N. and Shawn V. Lombardo. "The State of Streaming Video Content at Academic Libraires." *Collection Management*, 48, no. 4 (2023): 397-408. https://doi.org/10.1080/01462679.2 023.2255561.

Lobato, Ramon. *Netflix Nations: The Geography of Digital Distribution*. New York: New York University Press, 2019.

Loftis, Elsa and Carly Lamphere. "Swimming Upstream in the Academic Library: Exploring Faculty Needs for Library Streaming Media Collections." *Evidence Based Library and Information Practice*, 18, no. 4 (2023): 68-83.

MacDougall, Ruby and Dylan Ruediger. *Teaching with Streaming Video: Understanding Instructional Practices, Challenges, and Support Needs*. New York: Ithaka S+R, 2023. https://doi.org/10.18665/sr.318216.

McCormick, Casey. "'Forward is the Battle Cry': Binge-Viewing Netflix's House of Cards." In *The Netflix Effect: Technology and Entertainment in the 21st Century*, edited by Kevin McDonald and Daniel Smith-Rowsey, 101-116. New York: Bloomsbury Publishing, 2016.

Nielsen, Rasmus Kleis, and Sarah Anne Ganter. *The Power of Platforms: Shaping Media and Society*. New York: Oxford University Press, 2022.

Sim, Gerald. "Individual Disruptors and Economic Gamechangers: Netflix, New Media and Neoliberalism." In *The Netflix Effect: Technology and Entertainment in the 21st Century*, edited by Kevin McDonald and Daniel Smith-Rowsey, 186-201. New York: Bloomsbury Publishing, 2016.

Stelter, Brian. "New Way to Deliver a Drama: All 13 Episodes in One Sitting. *The New York Times*. February 1, 2013.

Stoll, Julia. "Estimated Number of SVOD Subscribers Worldwide from 2020 to 2029, by Service" in *Statista*, December 21, 2023. Accessed January 30, 2024, https://www.statista.com/statistics/1052770/global-svod-subscriber-count-by-platform/.

Tanasse, Gisèle. "Implementing and Managing Streaming Media Services in Academic Libraries." Chicago, IL: *ACRL/Choice*. 2021 https://www.choice360.org/research/implementing-and-managing-streaming-media-services-in-academic-libraries/.

Urban, Sandra Gall. "Evaluating Kanopy Access Models in Academic Libraries: Balancing Demand and Budget Constraints." *Collection Development* 47, no. 1 (2022): 37-48.

Vallier, John. "Twenty-First Century Academic Media Center: Killer App or Chindogu?" *Library Trends*, 58, no. 3 (Winter 2010): 378-390.

Writers Guild of America. *The New Gatekeepers: How Disney, Amazon, and Netflix will Take Over Media*. Los Angeles, CA: Writers Guild of America, 2023. Accessed December 2023, https://www.wga.org/uploadedfiles/news_and_events/public_policy/GatekeepersReport23.pdf.

Digital Heritage after Platformisation
Double Binds at Two Legal Deposit Libraries

Kieran Hegarty

This chapter examines the implications of platform power on library efforts to collect and provide access to the documentary heritage. Since at least the adoption of the *UNESCO Charter on the Preservation of the Digital Heritage* in 2003, it has been widely recognised that documentary heritage is increasingly digital in form.[1] "Digital heritage" is defined by UNESCO as "computer-based materials of enduring value that should be kept for future generations." These materials "are frequently ephemeral, and require purposeful production, maintenance and management to be retained."[2] Information produced and shared via the internet is at particular risk of loss. Websites and content shared on online platforms are regularly revised and edited, existing in a highly dynamic information

---

1   United Nations Educational, Scientific and Cultural Organisation, "Charter on the Preservation of Digital Heritage," 15 October 2003, http://portal.unesco.org/en/ev.php-URL_ID=17721&URL_DO=DO_TOPIC&URL_SECTION=201.html.

2   United Nations Educational, Scientific and Cultural Organisation, art. 1.

environment.³ In this context, libraries rapidly seek to collect a selection of this material for posterity "before dot-com becomes dot-gone."⁴

The commitment by libraries to collect and preserve online material has been further bolstered by the steady introduction of electronic legal deposit and the development of standards and automated technologies to support collecting processes.⁵ In this context, over 25 national libraries around the world have developed vast collections of publicly available web material, alongside the non-profit digital library the Internet Archive, which provides free, online access to hundreds of billions of archived web pages through its "Wayback Machine," along with non-institutional actors such as the Archive Team.⁶ Through the use of automated harvesting software, these web archives bring together copies of web pages, collected at

---

3   Fatih Oguz and Wallace Koehler, "URL Decay at Year 20: A Research Note," *Journal of the Association for Information Science and Technology* 67, no. 2 (2016): 477–79, https://doi.org/10.1002/asi.23561; Wallace Koehler, "A Longitudinal Study of Web Pages Continued: A Consideration of Document Persistence," *Information Research* 9, no. 2 (2014), http://informationr.net/ir/9-2/paper174.html; Joseph B. Bayer et al., "Sharing the Small Moments: Ephemeral Social Interaction on Snapchat," *Information, Communication & Society* 19, no. 7 (2016): 956–77, https://doi.org/10.1080/1369118X.2015.1084349.

4   Paul Koerbin, "Hit Save before Dot-Com Becomes Dot-Gone," *ABC News*, 8 May 2009, https://webarchive.nla.gov.au/awa/20180507173136/http://www.abc.net.au/news/2009-05-07/hit-save-before-dot-com-becomes-dot-gone/1674984.

5   Paul Gooding and Melissa Terras, *Electronic Legal Deposit: Shaping the Library Collections of the Future* (Facet, 2019); Peter Webster, "Users, Technologies, Organisations: Towards a Cultural History of World Web Archiving," in *Web 25: Histories from 25 Years of the World Wide Web*, ed. Niels Brügger (Bern, Switzerland: Peter Lang, 2017), 179–90.

6   Based on their 2010–2011 survey of web archiving initiatives, Gomes and colleagues created a Wikipedia page that is collaboratively kept up to date by those involved in web archiving around the world. See: Wikipedia contributors, "List of Web Archiving Initiatives," Wikipedia, 23 October 2020, https://en.wikipedia.org/w/index.php?title=List_of_Web_archiving_initiatives&oldid=984963799. For the original article see: Daniel Gomes, João Miranda, and Miguel Costa, "A Survey on Web Archiving Initiatives," in *International Conference on Theory and Practice of Digital Libraries*, ed. Stefan Gradmann et al., vol. 6966, *Lecture Notes in Computer Science* (Berlin, Heidelberg: Springer, 2011), 408–20, https://doi.org/10.1007/978-3-642-24469-8_41.

different times. Through their development, libraries seek to preserve a selective record of the web in perpetuity, capturing not only the content but also maintaining the functionality, look, and feel of a webpage as closely as possible to its original form.[7] Web archives are said to preserve "our common digital legacy"[8] or "our digital collective memory"[9] and therefore constitute "the web's memory organs."[10]

Platformisation: A New Challenge for Digital Heritage Preservation

The web has changed dramatically since the Internet Archive and several national libraries started their web archives in the mid-1990s. Whether we frame the history of the web as a series of "versions" (i.e. the move from web 1.0 to web 2.0 to web 3.0)[11] or an experiential shift from "surfing" in the 1990s to "searching" in the 2000s to "scrolling" in the 2010s,[12] there

---

7 International Organization for Standardization, "Information and Documentation—Statistics and Quality Issues for Web Archiving" (Geneva: International Organization for Standardization, 2013), para. 3, https://www.iso.org/obp/ui/#iso:std:iso:tr:14873:ed-1:v1:en; Society of American Archivists, "Web Archives," accessed 30 October 2023, https://dictionary.archivists.org/entry/web-archives.html.

8 William Kilbride, "Making History: Digital Preservation and Electronic Legal Deposit in the Second Quarter of the 21st Century," in *Electronic Legal Deposit*, ed. Paul Gooding and Melissa Terras, 1st ed. (Facet, 2019), 155, https://doi.org/10.29085/9781783303786.009.

9 Daniela Major and Daniel Gomes, "Web Archives Preserve Our Digital Collective Memory," in *The Past Web: Exploring Web Archives*, ed. Daniel Gomes et al. (Cham: Springer, 2021), 11–19, https://doi.org/10.1007/978-3-030-63291-5_2.

10 Anat Ben-David, "Critical Web Archive Research," in *The Past Web: Exploring Web Archives*, ed. Daniel Gomes et al. (Cham: Springer, 2021), 187, https://doi.org/10.1007/978-3-030-63291-5_14.

11 Matthew Allen, "What Was Web 2.0? Versions as the Dominant Mode of Internet History," *New Media & Society* 15, no. 2 (2013): 260–75, https://doi.org/10.1177/1461444812451567.

12 Richard Rogers, "Doing Web History with the Internet Archive: Screencast Documentaries," *Internet Histories* 1, no. 1–2 (2017): 161, https://doi.org/10.1080/24701475.2017.1307542.

is a general consensus that the web has moved from a relatively open, navigation-based information space to a more centralised environment dominated by a series of large commercial companies. This has both material and cultural consequences. The concept of "platformisation" has been used to describe both key technical-material changes in the way information moves around the web as well as the reorganisation of cultural practices and markets in the interests of large commercial platforms.[13] Describing the steady transition and ongoing tension between the "public-oriented Open Web" and the "locked-in 'walled gardens'" of platforms, Plantin and colleagues note that this process of platformisation entails "moving away from published URIs and open HTTP transactions in favor of closed apps that undertake hidden transactions with [platforms] through a [platform]-controlled API."[14] This "profit-motivated 'platformization'," they suggest, "is beginning to eat away at the foundational promise of the Open Web."[15] In this chapter, I examine how web archiving efforts are being challenged by this process of platformisation and its impact on what is collected and made available in web archives.

---

13 Helmond's foundational work on platformisation defines the process as "the extension of social media platforms into the rest of the web and their drive to make external web "platform ready."" Nieborg and Poell have used this concept to explore how the rise of platforms has reshaped cultural production, arguing that the shift to platforms as key sites of cultural production sees producers impelled to develop content in ways that align with the logic and interests of platforms. This, as Nielsen and Ganter discuss, has also had a major impact on publishers. See: Anne Helmond, "The Platformization of the Web: Making Web Data Platform Ready," *Social Media + Society* 1, no. 2 (2015): 1–11, https://doi.org/10.1177/2056305115603080; David Nieborg and Thomas Poell, "The Platformization of Cultural Production: Theorizing the Contingent Cultural Commodity," *New Media & Society* 20, no. 11 (2018): 4275–92, https://doi.org/10.1177/1461444818769694; Rasmus Kleis Nielsen and Sarah Anne Ganter, *The Power of Platforms: Shaping Media and Society* (Oxford University Press, 2022).

14 Jean-Christophe Plantin et al., "Infrastructure Studies Meet Platform Studies in the Age of Google and Facebook," *New Media & Society* 20, no. 1 (2018): 301–303, https://doi.org/10.1177/1461444816661553.

15 Plantin et al., "Infrastructure," 303.

This chapter draws on ethnographic and historical research at two legal deposit libraries; the National Library of Australia (NLA) and the oldest library in Australia, the State Library of New South Wales (SLNSW). Both libraries have legislated collecting mandates.[16] The NLA was one of the first libraries in the world to start a web archiving program, commencing their PANDORA web archive in 1996 (now called the Australian Web Archive).[17] The SLNSW has a responsibility to collect material relevant to Australia's most populous state and has maintained a specific Social Media Archive since 2012.[18] Through interviews with library workers, observing and participating in everyday work practices, and analysis of organisational records, I sought to understand the impact of platformisation on their efforts to collect and provide access to the documentary heritage at national and state levels.

I will illustrate how, to collect selected content from large social media platforms such as Facebook and Twitter (now X), major public libraries such as the NLA and SLNSW find themselves with two limited and limiting choices—a "double bind."[19] The first option, taken by the NLA, is to resist platform-sanctioned mechanisms for collecting social media content and

---

16 The National Library of Australia is directed "to maintain and develop a national collection of library material, including a comprehensive collection of library material relating to Australia and the Australian people" (National Library Act 1960, Sect. 6a) and the State Library of New South Wales is "to identify relevant library material, to collect relevant library material [and] to maintain relevant library material as part of the collection of the library" (Libraries Act 1939, sect. 14B).

17 See: https://webarchive.nla.gov.au/.

18 Kathryn Barwick et al., "Hunters and Collectors: Seeking Social Media Content for Cultural Heritage Collections," in VALA2014: Streaming with Possibilities (Melbourne: VALA, 2014), http://www.vala.org.au/vala2014-proceedings/vala2014-session-7-barwick. See: https://socialmediaarchive.sl.nsw.gov.au/.

19 Kim Fortun et al., "Civic Community Archiving with the Platform for Experimental Collaborative Ethnography: Double Binds and Design Challenges," in *Culture and Computing. Design Thinking and Cultural Computing*, ed. Matthias Rauterberg, Lecture Notes in Computer Science (Cham: Springer, 2021), 36–55, https://doi.org/10.1007/978-3-030-77431-8_3.

attempt to collect this content using "web crawling" techniques used to collect other parts of the web.[20] The benefit of this approach is that content collected through web crawling can usually be made immediately accessible. However, platforms often block web crawling software, meaning staff must come up with short-term workarounds or suffice with incomplete or inconsistent captures.[21]

The second approach to collecting content from large social media platforms involves the use of application programming interfaces (APIs), which allow the extraction of structured data from the platform according to certain criteria.[22] This is the approach taken by the SLNSW with their Social Media Archive. This option, too, has drawbacks. The use of APIs ties data collection and use to a shifting set of terms of conditions that limit how these data can be used, which can significantly challenge library mandates that direct them to provide public access to their collections.[23] Moreover, the amount and type of data gathered with platform APIs is opaque and can change, often drastically, as seen in the post-Facebook–Cambridge Analytica data scandal "APIcalypse"[24] and the radical, post-Musk

---

20 Niels Brügger, *The Archived Web: Doing History in the Digital Age* (Cambridge: MIT Press, 2018).

21 Anat Ben-David, "Counter-Archiving Facebook," *European Journal of Communication* 35, no. 3 (2020): 249–64, https://doi.org/10.1177/0267323120922069.

22 Stine Lomborg and Anja Bechmann, "Using APIs for Data Collection on Social Media," *The Information Society* 30, no. 4 (2014): 256–65, https://doi.org/10.1080/01972243.2014.915276.

23 Kieran Hegarty, "Unlocking Social Media Archives: Creative Responses to the Challenge of Access," in *VALA2022: Bring IT On!* (Melbourne: VALA, 2022), https://researchrepository.rmit.edu.au/esploro/outputs/9922159378501341.

24 The Facebook–Cambridge Analytica data scandal involved the unauthorised harvesting of Facebook user data by Cambridge Analytica, a political consulting firm, which was used in an attempt to influence the 2016 US presidential election. For a discussion on the impact of these changes on academic research, see: Axel Bruns, "After the 'APIcalypse': Social Media Platforms and Their Fight against Critical Scholarly Research," *Information, Communication & Society* 22, no. 11 (2019): 1544–66, https://doi.org/10.1080/1369118X.2019.1637447.

changes to the Twitter API.[25] Both of these examples serve to illustrate the power of platforms to establish (and thereby change) the conditions that enable and constrain flows of information hosted on their services into library collections.

Web Crawling in the Age of Social Media Platforms

"Things like Facebook, I think, are deliberately built to avoid being archived." I am speaking to Russell, a Web Archivist at the NLA. Russell has worked at the library since 2006—the same year Twitter was created and Facebook was made publicly available. In May and June 2021, I observed and participated in the work of Russell and his colleagues in the library's Web Archiving Section. After our discussion ended, I reviewed the library's attempts to collect Facebook content. While there is some Facebook content in the Australian Web Archive, much of it is inconsistent—an event page here, a public profile there—and incomplete. I located a snapshot of a page from February 2021. It shows me a blank white page with the trademarked platform name written in lower-case blue text on the top left, as if guarding the entrance to its territory. The rest of the page appears empty.

This patchy crawl of a Facebook page illustrates the issues libraries have in attempting to collect and preserve platform content. While there are many forms of web archiving, collecting institutions often rely on "web crawling," a sophisticated

---

25 The acquisition of the microblogging platform Twitter by business magnate Elon Musk in 2022 led to significant changes in strategy, branding, and direction at the company, including a drastic increase in API access costs. The new API pricing, introduced in early 2023, starts at $500,000 annually for limited data access, a change from the previously free access essential for academic research. See: Ivan Mehta and Manish Singh, "Twitter to End Free Access to Its API in Elon Musk's Latest Monetization Push," *TechCrunch* (blog), 2 February 2023, https://techcrunch.com/2023/02/01/twitter-to-end-free-access-to-its-api/; Chris Stokel-Walker, "Twitter's $42,000-per-Month API Prices Out Nearly Everyone," *Wired*, 10 March 2023, https://www.wired.com/story/twitter-data-api-prices-out-nearly-everyone/.

and scalable way to collect and preserve web material.[26] Web crawling uses dedicated software (called "crawlers" or "harvesters") that allows the archiving agent to insert a list of web addresses (URLs), the files and code of which are gathered along with metadata associated with the crawling process. Given that the intention of web archiving is to replay webpages as they existed in a live web environment, the crawler follows all links on the specified page and gathers that content where possible. This recursive process continues until ceasing for various reasons—whether specified in the software, due to an error, or the crawler has started collecting content deemed irrelevant to the archiving agent. Web crawling has enabled libraries to preserve terabytes of material in web archives, some of which are openly accessible, including the Internet Archive's Wayback Machine and the web archives of the Australian, Croatian, and Portuguese national libraries.[27]

However, web crawling has its limits. Site owners can embed the Robots Exclusion Protocol (robots.txt) in the site's code, which instructs the web crawler where on the website it can and cannot visit.[28] More pressingly, anything requiring user authentication (e.g. a CAPTCHA code, a password, or IP authentication) will essentially stop the crawler in its tracks. Really, any form of user interaction apart from clicking on a link can impede the crawler's journey through the web. Social media poses a particular problem for the NLA's collecting techniques. Facebook, for example, is largely closed to crawlers, and the platform has policies and license agreements that prohibit the

---

26 Brügger, *The Archived Web*.

27 Niels Brügger, "Digital Humanities and Web Archives: Possible New Paths for Combining Datasets," *International Journal of Digital Humanities* 2, no. 1 (2021): 145–68, https://doi.org/10.1007/s42803-021-00038-z.

28 The Robots Exclusion Protocol relies on voluntary compliance. Some web archives (such as the Internet Archive's Wayback Machine) respect robots.txt, while others, particularly legal deposit libraries, choose not to.

use of "harvesting bots, robots, spiders, or scrapers...without Facebook's express written permission."[29] A NLA Web Archiving Section monthly report from 2016 noted, "Facebook does not harvest.... It instantly recognises the harvester as a robot and puts a CAPTCHA block up."

In response to the challenges associated with collecting social media using web crawling, Russell and his colleagues engage in workarounds in an attempt to gather material that falls within the library's broad collecting remit. These workarounds change as the library tries to keep ahead of ongoing changes to platform design and policies. Take Twitter—until recently one of the more permissive platforms in terms of providing third parties access to platform data.[30] Russell told me, "We used to collect Twitter quite a bit... Twitter was the only [social media platform] that was in some way archivable." Collecting Twitter at the NLA was achieved—for a period—through a series of creative workarounds. Generally, attempts to crawl Twitter profiles were blocked or resulted in error-filled crawls. However, library staff discovered that collecting the *mobile* version of Twitter pages was possible. After showing twenty posts, the mobile version of a Twitter profile, for a time, had a *Load older Tweets* button (see Figure 1). The harvester could capture these profiles because "that's what a harvester does, it follows links," as Russell explained. The eventual fate of this workaround, and many like it, illustrates who has the power to decide what material can be archived by libraries. After successfully using the "mobile Twitter" workaround for several years, the design of Twitter's mobile site changed in December 2020. Gone was the *Load older Tweets* button which linked to

---

29 Facebook, "Automated Data Collection Terms," 15 April 2010, https://www.facebook.com/apps/site_scraping_tos_terms.php.

30 Jean Burgess and Axel Bruns, "Easy Data, Hard Data: The Politics and Pragmatics of Twitter Research after the Computational Turn," in *Compromised Data: From Social Media to Big Data*, ed. G. Elmer, J. Redden, and G. Langlois (Bloomsbury, 2015), 93–111.

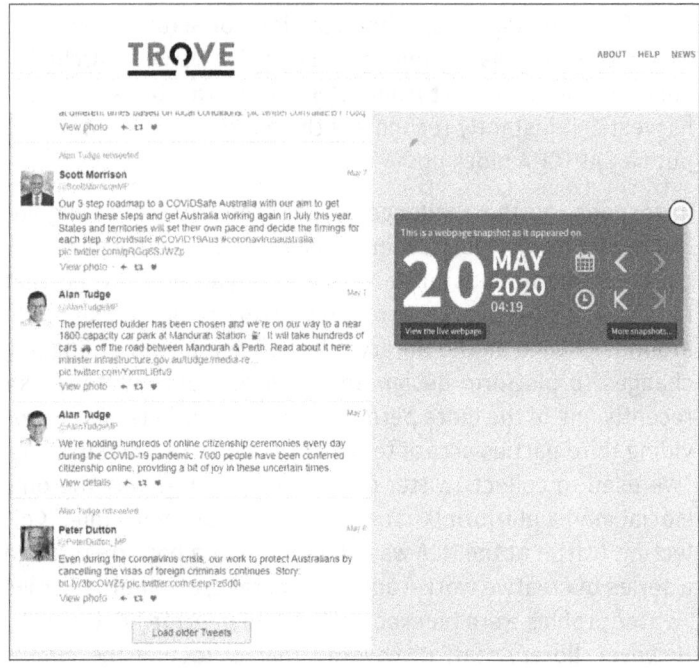

Figure 1   Former government minister and parliamentarian Alan Tudge (@AlanTudgeMP) on Twitter. Note the "Load older Tweets" button at the bottom of the page, allowing the NLA to use a web crawler to periodically collect Tudge's tweets and retweets. Retrieved 20 May 2020 04:19 (source: Australian Web Archive).

the next page. Users of Twitter's mobile interface would now scroll to retrieve more Tweets (rather than click the *Load older Tweets* button). Not only that—"they changed something else" as well, meaning the library "couldn't even get the first page," as Russell explained. While the NLA tends to discard these error-filled attempts, an example in the Wayback Machine shows the results of trying to use web crawling to capture the page seen in Figure 1 (see Figure 2). The rationale, nature, and timing of the change were unclear to Russell and his colleagues, but

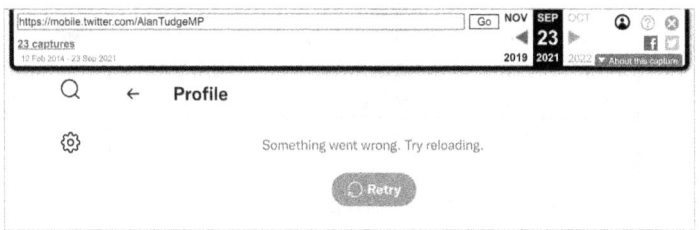

Figure 2 An error-filled attempt to gather former government minister and parliamentarian Alan Tudge's (@AlanTudgeMP) Twitter profile on 23 September 2021. The attempted capture was made after the design of Twitter's mobile site changed in December 2020, meaning a workaround used by web archivists to gather the page no longer worked (source: Internet Archive's Wayback Machine).

the results are clear—the harvests simply no longer worked.[31] The result is inconsistent collections, filled with unexpected ruptures that are left underexplained to both library workers and users of web archives alike.

The power relations between platforms and libraries, as they are with all third parties, are deeply unequal.[32] This is illustrated in a 2010 exchange between the NLA and Facebook. As mentioned, NLA is a public institution with a long-standing legislative mandate to develop and provide ongoing access to comprehensive national collections. Despite this, the library has little bargaining power over large digital platforms like Facebook. To overcome the inability to collect material from

---

31 Since this change, Twitter pages were not collected for an extended period, until the library discovered it could collect pages using a free and open-source alternative viewer for Twitter called Nitter. However, after Twitter transitioned to X in 2022, third parties who relied on free API access to build products like Nitter faced increasing restrictions, and the service was officially discontinued in early 2024. With this closure, another of the NLA's workarounds was curtailed.

32 Nielsen and Ganter, *Power*.

the platform, the library sought permission from Facebook in 2010 to collect and make available then-Australian Prime Minister Julia Gillard's Facebook page. Given the NLA's long history of collecting Australian prime ministers' personal papers, diaries, oral histories, and websites,[1] the page seems well within the library's scope of collecting. Yet, Facebook's response to the NLA's request shows who has the power to decide what is retrieved from platform environments, and on what terms. The reply from a Facebook representative read:

> So long as you follow our Developer Policies and utilize the proper APIs and other technology made available by Facebook…you could archive the Pages required. This means using our approved APIs and technology and not scraping or other technologies.

After the library responded, clarifying their collecting responsibilities and what they intended to do with the archived page, Facebook came back:

> Our rules are very clear on this and it sounds like your system might violate the Facebook terms. [You] can look at our Facebook Developer Site or our Automated Terms to ensure any actions [you] take [are] compliant with Facebook's terms. Again *it is possible to archive these pages but only if you follow Facebook's terms.*[2]

---

1 Paul Koerbin, "To Know, to Utter, to Argue…and to Archive and Access: What Place Does Archived Online Content Have in Social Media's Political Discourse? Part 2 of 2," *National Library of Australia Blog* (blog), 27 May 2014, https://webarchive.nla.gov.au/awa/20160719061925/., https://www.nla.gov.au/blogs/web-archiving/2014/05/27/to-know-to-utter-to-argue-and-to-archive-and-access; National Library of Australia, "Menzies Collection," *National Library of Australia*, 2019, https://www.nla.gov.au/collections/guide-selected-collections/menzies-collection.

2 Emphasis added.

This interaction between an established public institution and a large social media company neatly illustrates the changing levels of control that different entities have over the collection, distribution, and use of information. Yet, utilising "the proper APIs and other technologies" made available by platforms has its own drawbacks that further illustrate the power of platforms to set the rules that social media users and "third parties" like libraries have to follow, as we shall see in the next section.

API-Based Collecting: Navigating Platform Constraints

There is an alternative to the workarounds deployed by Russell and his colleagues at the NLA in their ongoing efforts to collect material from social media platforms using web crawling. Platforms do offer official channels to guide flows of data out of, and into, platform environments. APIs, designed by platforms, give external users (so-called third parties) controlled access to their services and data. Among these third parties are developers, who use the API to build platform-specific applications; academic researchers, who use social media data as research data; advertisers, who use APIs to analyse data and target users with advertisements; and "stewards" such as collecting institutions, who use APIs to collect social media data for long-term preservation and use.[3] From the platform's perspective, the aim of attracting third parties is to add value to a platform by improving the user experience, attracting more users, encouraging engagement, and enabling more granular user profiles to be created and sold to advertisers to target users. Helmond suggests that it is this offer of APIs that

---

3   Amelia Acker and Adam Kreisberg, "Social Media Data Archives in an API-Driven World," *Archival Science* 20, no. 2 (2020): 105–23, https://doi.org/10.1007/s10502-019-09325-9.

defines platforms, noting that "the moment social network *sites* offer APIs, they turn into social media *platforms* by enacting their programmability."[4] While developers are the main target audience for APIs,[5] these access points also enable other users, such as researchers or collecting institutions, to gather social media data. Through the use of APIs, libraries could theoretically access streams of social media data, which might include profile information, posts, number of "likes" or "shares," and other metadata based on specific queries or criteria (e.g. a hashtag, keyword, or user).

Paul, one of Russell's colleagues in the Web Archiving Section, has worked in the field since the library started its web archiving efforts in 1996 and firmly believes that "without access, preservation is little more than a costly and meaningless storage burden."[6] At the NLA, as Paul and I looked at yet another error-filled attempt to collect a public figure's Twitter profile (this time a well-known Australian journalist), I asked him if the library had considered using the Twitter API, given the unpredictability of collecting this content using crawlers. "They [Twitter] won't give us an API," Paul answered. I ask him why not. "We were honest and told them what we were going to use it for," he explained. Access to social media data using APIs is governed by platforms and their terms of service agreements.[7] According to the terms set out in Twitter's *Developer Policy* in use while I was on fieldwork in 2021, "if Twitter Content is

---

4   Helmond, "The Platformization of the Web," 4. Emphasis added.

5   Rebekah Tromble, "Where Have All the Data Gone? A Critical Reflection on Academic Digital Research in the Post-API Age," *Social Media + Society* 7, no. 1 (2021), https://doi.org/10.1177/2056305121988929.

6   Paul Koerbin, "Revisiting the World Wide Web as Artefact: Case Studies in Archiving Small Data for the National Library of Australia's PANDORA Archive," in *Web 25: Histories from 25 Years of the World Wide Web*, ed. Niels Brügger (Bern, Switzerland: Peter Lang, 2017), 195.

7   Acker and Kreisberg, "Social."

deleted, gains protected status, or is otherwise suspended, withheld, modified, or removed...you will make all reasonable efforts to delete or modify such Twitter Content."[8] "You have to abide by their conditions," Paul said, referencing this clause in the policy, "if the Tweets are taken down, you've got to take it down. That's not *archiving* as far as I'm concerned." "I just don't see the value," Paul continued. "What are we going to do with it? Collect it, but not make it available?" Given the provision of access to their collections is "the quintessential raison d'etre of libraries,"[9] Paul "can't...see the payoff" in collecting social media using APIs. Here we can see fundamental fissures emerge between the commercial priorities and interests of the platforms and the goals and values of libraries.

Official Access Points and Their Discontents

While the NLA has been reluctant to adopt API-based social media collecting as a supplement to web crawling, the SLNSW has taken this path since 2012 with its Social Media Archive.[10] Using APIs reconfigures how library collections are formed, and what can be done with them.[11] The combination of APIs and terms of service agreements condition what is collected and how it is collected, as well as shaping if and how

---

[8] Justin Littman, "Twitter's Developer Policies for Researchers, Archivists, and Librarians," On *Archivy* (blog), 8 January 2019, https://medium.com/on-archivy/twitters-developer-policies-for-researchers-archivists-and-librarians-63e9ba0433b2. Chapter 2 of the current X Developer Policy contains similar provisions: https://developer.twitter.com/en/developer-terms/policy (accessed 21 January 2024).

[9] Helena Robinson, "Remembering Things Differently: Museums, Libraries and Archives as Memory Institutions and the Implications for Convergence," *Museum Management and Curatorship* 27, no. 4 (2012): 416, https://doi.org/10.1080/09647775.2012.720188.

[10] Barwick et al., "Hunters."

[11] Kevin Driscoll and Shawn Walker, "Working Within a Black Box: Transparency in the Collection and Production of Big Twitter Data," *International Journal of Communication* 8 (2014).

collected material can be made accessible. As has been well documented, APIs can change radically, or be shut down altogether, as seen in 2018, when the API for the popular photo and video-sharing platform Instagram was suddenly shut down.[12] Meanwhile, licence agreements that govern the use of APIs can change, often reinforcing technical changes to APIs.[13] Thus, an evolving "governance arrangement,"[14] combining licence agreements and API design, significantly influences how social media data can be used and shared, shifting the decision-making power over library collections from public institutions to private companies.

API-based social media collecting at the SLNSW started in 2012, well before the Facebook–Cambridge Analytica data scandal in 2018 and the post-Musk takeover of Twitter in 2022 that saw API access curbed considerably. While aware of the legal and ethical constraints of providing access to content captured from social media platforms, the project leader of the Social Media Archive was "very conscious that if we didn't collect it, it would be gone." She told me in an interview, "even if we had to collect it and lock it away for fifty years…it would [still] be important to collect." I have described two paths taken by Australia's major public libraries to collect material from social media platforms—patchy, error-ridden crawls, collected through precarious workarounds, that can nonetheless be made immediately available on the terms of the library; or the systematic collection of structured platform data and

---

12 Bruns, "After"; Josh Constine, "Facebook Restricts APIs, Axes Old Instagram Platform amidst Scandals," *TechCrunch* (blog), 5 April 2018, https://techcrunch.com/2018/04/04/facebook-instagram-api-shut-down.

13 Anne Helmond, David B. Nieborg, and Fernando N. van der Vlist, "Facebook's Evolution: Development of a Platform-as-Infrastructure," *Internet Histories* 3, no. 2 (2019): 123–46, https://doi.org/10.1080/24701475.2019.1593667; Fernando N. van der Vlist et al., "API Governance: The Case of Facebook's Evolution," *Social Media + Society* 8, no. 2 (2022), https://doi.org/10.1177/20563051221086228.

14 van der Vlist et al., "API Governance," 2.

metadata, where access is deferred to some indeterminate future when the various technical, legal, and ethical issues surrounding access are resolved.

For the SLNSW, APIs undoubtedly enabled social media content—particularly Twitter content—to be collected more systematically than is possible using web crawling.[15] Consider the inconsistent crawls of Facebook pages and Twitter profiles that I highlighted earlier, or the laborious and precarious workarounds undertaken to capture even a remotely analogous version of this content. API-based collecting, on the other hand, returns structured social media data. However, as one of my interviewees involved in the SLNSW Social Media Archive confessed to me in 2021, "we're at the mercy of the platforms to a certain degree…the ramifications of API changes mean what may have been practical to do five years ago is no longer." While API use enables a platform-sanctioned way to collect social media data, the companies that own these services can change the design of APIs and the terms that govern their use. For example, Facebook's APIs have frequently changed, with each change reflecting the priorities and interests of the company.[16] Twitter, which previously had offered more permissive access than Facebook, recently curtailed free API access and introduced substantial costs for developers and researchers to move beyond basic use cases as part of a series of dramatic changes at the company.[17]

---

15 After two years of collecting, the library had collected around 6.7 million instances, 94.6% of which were from Twitter. See: State Library of New South Wales, "Digital Collecting Strategy" (Sydney: State Library of New South Wales, 2014), https://www.sl.nsw.gov.au/sites/default/files/digital_collecting_strategy_version_1.0_-_8_december_2014.pdf.

16 Helmond, Nieborg, and van der Vlist, "Facebook's Evolution."

17 Stokel-Walker, "Twitter's $42,000-per-Month API."

As platform studies scholars have noted, different API users are also provided with different levels of service and support.[18] This means that both the content retrieved, and what can be done with it, are in a constant state of flux, changing according to the priorities of the platform. One of my interviewees, who works on the technical infrastructure for the SLNSW Social Media Archive, reflected on far-reaching changes that occurred in 2018, following the Facebook–Cambridge Analytica data scandal:

> Really difficult things happened in 2018.... Facebook suddenly dropped their search APIs and also reduced the rate limit...Twitter suddenly dropped time zone information and other profile information. [The] Instagram API merged into the Facebook API. Then it's really hard to get some geolocation information from Instagram... they reduced the rate limit significantly as well. It was really a hard time for us since there was so many changes in the social media platforms.

By embarking on API-based social media collecting, the contemporaneous collection of material available online is therefore constrained and enabled by platform strategies for governing how social media content can be created, distributed, and used.[19] Through the offer of APIs, platforms simultaneously open up new opportunities for developing library collections, while also controlling what data are collected and how these data can be made accessible to library users.

---

18 Nicholas A. John and Asaf Nissenbaum, "An Agnotological Analysis of APIs: Or, Disconnectivity and the Ideological Limits of Our Knowledge of Social Media," *The Information Society* 35, no. 1 (January 2019): 1–12, https://doi.org/10.1080/01972243.2018.1542647.

19 Tarleton Gillespie, "Regulation of and by Platforms," in *The SAGE Handbook of Social Media*, by Jean Burgess, Alice Marwick, and Thomas Poell (London: SAGE, 2018), 254–78, https://doi.org/10.4135/9781473984066.n15.

Conclusion: Resisting Platformisation Through Counter-Archiving

When considering how to collect and provide access to social media content, Australia's national and state libraries find themselves in a "double binding situation"; the product of "incompatible, contradictory statements or demands that can neither be avoided nor resolved."[20] This is illustrated in the fact that while the NLA can (and sometimes does) provide public access to its inconsistent, error-prone crawls of Facebook pages, the SLNSW cannot (or does not) provide granular access to the vast amount of structured data collected they have collected through various social media APIs. Instead, they use data visualisation to illustrate dominant hashtags and keywords presently being posted.[21] While SLNSW staff I interviewed acknowledged this was limited, at least "there's a bit of stuff that people can look at," one told me. The platform-centred conditions imposed on API clients directly conflict with the goals and interests of libraries, including "the *sine qua non* purpose of archiving and preservation: sustainable long term access."[22] Given the constraints on collection and access imposed through API design and the license agreements that govern their use, libraries are forced to "put it in a box for 50 years...and let it mature," as one SLNSW staff member told me in an interview, effectively ceding control to platform interests.

Dependence on APIs, and the limits of web crawling in platform environments, raise critical questions about the autonomy of libraries tasked with collecting, preserving, and providing access to the documentary heritage in the long-term

---

20 Fortun et al., "Civic," 50.

21 Hegarty, "Unlocking."

22 Koerbin, "Revisiting," 195.

public interest. When libraries use APIs, they effectively cede control over what they can collect and how they can use the collected data. Platforms, through the design of their services and tools and the terms that govern their use, dictate terms of engagement that reflect their business models, rather than libraries' needs around collection, preservation, and access. Recall the email sent to the NLA by Facebook in response to their request to collect an Australian Prime Minister's Facebook page—"it is possible to archive these pages *but only if you follow Facebook's terms.*"[23] This reflects a power dynamic where the platforms exert significant influence over the content and form of library collections, restricting what can be collected, what can be done with them, who has access, and under what conditions.

In response to platformisation and the limits of APIs, researchers have started deriding the data made available by platforms through their APIs and are pushing back against platform-sanctioned mechanisms for collecting data. "Counter-archiving," has been proposed by digital media scholar Anat Ben-David as "a form of epistemic resistance" that questions the hegemonic order of platforms.[24] Counter-archiving involves archiving digital content in a way that challenges or counteracts the gaps, limitations and biases inherent in collecting platform content through official access points. This concept arises from the recognition that traditional collecting processes, often influenced by the policies of dominant online platforms, can lead to significant gaps and biases in the historical record.[25] Counter-archiving emphasises the ac-

---

23 Emphasis added.

24 Ben-David, "Counter-Archiving Facebook," 251.

25 Kieran Hegarty, "Representing Biases, Inequalities and Silences in National Web Archives: Social, Material and Technical Dimensions," *Archives & Manuscripts* 50, no. 1 (2022): 31–45, https://doi.org/10.37683/asa.v50.10209.

tive, selective preservation of content that may be overlooked or intentionally excluded by dominant archiving practices. It seeks to bypass or challenge the limitations imposed by large platforms on what can be archived and engages with communities to ensure a more representative digital heritage. Moreover, counter-archiving takes a critical perspective on collecting processes themselves, questioning who gets to decide what is worth preserving and highlighting the political and ethical dimensions of these decisions. Counter-archiving, therefore, is not just a technical process but also a political and ethical orientation toward the collection, preservation, and distribution of information. While this approach has long been pursued by citizen journalists and community activists such as the Archive Team, this approach also provides a model for libraries responsible for digital heritage after platformisation.

After platformisation, the rules that shape information flows are increasingly enforced through technologies and reflect the interests of private corporations. This means that the contents of library collections are often contingent on corporate policies and technologies that determine what can be accessed and how. As a recent submission on behalf of the Australian library sector to a government inquiry into the influence of international digital platforms noted, "libraries are no longer able to collect the full range of Australian documentary heritage… Australia's cultural memory is increasingly dependent on the whims of international platforms."[26] Given that library associations are reflecting an increasingly strident tone, and many researchers and social media users are growing wary of platform power, now is the time for libraries to unite with researchers and users to challenge the existing order. Rather

---

[26] Australian Library and Information Association and National and State Libraries Australasia, "ALIA-NSLA Submission to the Inquiry into the Influence of International Digital Platforms," March 2023, 3, https://read.alia.org.au/alia-nsla-submission-inquiry-influence-international-digital-platforms-march-2023.

than harvesting data using automated or platform-sanctioned means, libraries need to collect in the public interest, allowing the powerful to be held to account by collecting their digital records, prioritising those records prone to change or deletion.[27] Meanwhile, libraries should partner with a wide set of users to collect social media content, while ensuring user rights around consent and privacy are respected. This could involve data donation, as seen in AlgorithmWatch's #Datenspende project conducted during the 2017 German federal election,[28] or the Australian Search Experience project, which allows researchers and users alike to track what ads are being served up on social media platforms.[29] Through crowd-sourced mechanisms like these, libraries can ensure digital heritage reflects a wide public interest and experience, rather than the crumbs left behind by powerful platforms.

---

27 Katie Burgess, "Trove Used to Cast Doubt on Angus Taylor's Claims about Clover Moore Letter," *The Canberra Times*, 12 November 2019, https://www.canberratimes.com.au/story/6487619/trove-used-to-cast-doubt-on-angus-taylors-claims-about-clover-moore-letter/; Randeep Ramesh and Alex Hern, "Conservative Party Deletes Archive of Speeches from Internet," *The Guardian*, 13 November 2013, https://www.theguardian.com/politics/2013/nov/13/conservative-party-archive-speeches-internet; Coral Davenport, "With Trump in Charge, Climate Change References Purged From Website," *The New York Times*, 21 January 2017, https://www.nytimes.com/2017/01/20/us/politics/trump-white-house-website.html.

28 Tobias D. Krafft, Michael Gamer, and Katharina A. Zweig, "What Did You See? A Study to Measure Personalization in Google's Search Engine," *EPJ Data Science* 8, no. 1 (2019): 38, https://doi.org/10.1140/epjds/s13688-019-0217-5.

29 Axel Bruns, "Australian Search Experience Project: Background Paper," Report (ARC Centre of Excellence for Automated Decision-Making and Society, 15 January 2022), Australia, https://apo.org.au/node/316976.

Bibliography

Acker, Amelia, and Adam Kreisberg. "Social Media Data Archives in an API-Driven World." *Archival Science* 20, no. 2 (2020): 105–23. https://doi.org/10.1007/s10502-019-09325-9.

Allen, Matthew. "What Was Web 2.0? Versions as the Dominant Mode of Internet History." *New Media & Society* 15, no. 2 (2013): 260–75. https://doi.org/10.1177/1461444812451567.

Australian Government. National Library Act 1960 (1960).

Australian Library and Information Association and National and State Libraries Australasia. "ALIA-NSLA Submission to the Inquiry into the Influence of International Digital Platforms," March 2023. https://read.alia.org.au/alia-nsla-submission-inquiry-influence-international-digital-platforms-march-2023.

Barwick, Kathryn, Mylee Joseph, Cecile Paris, and Stephen Wan. "Hunters and Collectors: Seeking Social Media Content for Cultural Heritage Collections." In *VALA2014: Streaming with Possibilities*. Melbourne: VALA, 2014. http://www.vala.org.au/vala2014-proceedings/vala2014-session-7-barwick.

Bayer, Joseph B., Nicole B. Ellison, Sarita Y. Schoenebeck, and Emily B. Falk. "Sharing the Small Moments: Ephemeral Social Interaction on Snapchat." *Information, Communication & Society* 19, no. 7 (2016): 956–77. https://doi.org/10.1080/1369118X.2015.1084349.

Ben-David, Anat. "Counter-Archiving Facebook." *European Journal of Communication* 35, no. 3 (2020): 249–64. https://doi.org/10.1177/0267323120922069.

Ben-David, Anat. "Critical Web Archive Research." In *The Past Web: Exploring Web Archives*, edited by Daniel Gomes, Elena Demidova, Jane Winters, and Thomas Risse, 181–88. Cham: Springer, 2021. https://doi.org/10.1007/978-3-030-63291-5_14.

Brügger, Niels. "Digital Humanities and Web Archives: Possible New Paths for Combining Datasets." *International Journal of Digital Humanities* 2, no. 1 (2021): 145–68. https://doi.org/10.1007/s42803-021-00038-z.

Brügger, Niels. *The Archived Web: Doing History in the Digital Age*. Cambridge: MIT Press, 2018.

Bruns, Axel. "After the "APIcalypse": Social Media Platforms and Their Fight against Critical Scholarly Research." *Information, Communication & Society* 22, no. 11 (2019): 1544–66. https://doi.org/10.1080/1369118X.2019.1637447.

Bruns, Axel. "Australian Search Experience Project: Background Paper." Report. ARC Centre of Excellence for Automated Decision-Making and Society, 15 January 2022. Australia. https://apo.org.au/node/316976.

Burgess, Jean, and Axel Bruns. "Easy Data, Hard Data: The Politics and Pragmatics of Twitter Research after the Computational Turn." In *Compromised Data: From Social Media to Big Data*, edited by G. Elmer, J. Redden, and G. Langlois, 93–111. Bloomsbury, 2015.

Burgess, Katie. "Trove Used to Cast Doubt on Angus Taylor's Claims about Clover Moore Letter." *The Canberra Times*, 12 November 2019. https://www.canberratimes.com.au/story/6487619/trove-used-to-cast-doubt-on-angus-taylors-claims-about-clover-moore-letter/.

Constine, Josh. "Facebook Restricts APIs, Axes Old Instagram Platform amidst Scandals." *TechCrunch* (blog), 5 April 2018. https://techcrunch.com/2018/04/04/facebook-instagram-api-shut-down.

Crescentini, Noemi, Kieran Hegarty, Giuseppe M. Padricelli, Bernhard Rieder, and C. J. Reynolds. "Mapping Regimes of Data Access: Positioning Researchers in Platform Ecologies." Digital Methods Initiative, 2022. https://wiki.digitalmethods.net/Dmi/MappingRegimesOfDataAccessToS.

Davenport, Coral. "With Trump in Charge, Climate Change References Purged From Website." *The New York Times*, 21 January 2017. https://www.nytimes.com/2017/01/20/us/politics/trump-white-house-website.html.

Driscoll, Kevin, and Shawn Walker. "Big Data, Big Questions | Working Within a Black Box: Transparency in the Collection and Production of Big Twitter Data." *International Journal of Communication* 8 (2014): 20.

Espley, Suzy, Florent Carpentier, Radu Pop, and Leïla Medjkoune. "Collect, Preserve, Access: Applying the Governing Principles of the National Archives UK Government Web Archive to Social Media Content." *Alexandria* 25, no. 1–2 (2014): 31–50. https://doi.org/10.7227/ALX.0019.

Facebook. "Automated Data Collection Terms," 15 April 2010. https://www.facebook.com/apps/site_scraping_tos_terms.php.

Fortun, Kim, Mike Fortun, Angela Hitomi Skye Crandall Okune, Tim Schütz, and Shan-Ya Su. "Civic Community Archiving with the Platform for Experimental Collaborative Ethnography: Double Binds and Design Challenges." In *Culture and Computing. Design Thinking and Cultural Computing*, edited by Matthias Rauterberg, 36–55. Lecture Notes in Computer Science. Cham: Springer, 2021. https://doi.org/10.1007/978-3-030-77431-8_3.

Gillespie, Tarleton. "Regulation of and by Platforms." In *The SAGE Handbook of Social Media*, by Jean Burgess, Alice Marwick, and Thomas Poell, 254–78. London: SAGE, 2018. https://doi.org/10.4135/9781473984066.n15.

Daniel Gomes, João Miranda, and Miguel Costa, "A Survey on Web Archiving Initiatives," in *International Conference on Theory and Practice of Digital Libraries*, ed. Stefan Gradmann et al., vol. 6966, Lecture Notes in Computer Science (Berlin, Heidelberg: Springer, 2011), 408–20, https://doi.org/10.1007/978-3-642-24469-8_41.

Gooding, Paul, and Melissa Terras. *Electronic Legal Deposit: Shaping the Library Collections of the Future*. Facet, 2019.

Hegarty, Kieran. "Representing Biases, Inequalities and Silences in National Web Archives: Social, Material and Technical Dimensions." *Archives & Manuscripts* 50, no. 1 (2022): 31–45. https://doi.org/10.37683/asa.v50.10209.

Hegarty, Kieran. "Unlocking Social Media Archives: Creative Responses to the Challenge of Access." In *VALA2022: Bring IT On!* Melbourne: VALA, 2022. https://researchrepository.rmit.edu.au/esploro/outputs/9922159378501341.

Helmond, Anne. "The Platformization of the Web: Making Web Data Platform Ready." *Social Media + Society* 1, no. 2 (2015): 1–11. https://doi.org/10.1177/2056305115603080.

Helmond, Anne, David B. Nieborg, and Fernando N. van der Vlist. "Facebook's Evolution: Development of a Platform-as-Infrastructure." *Internet Histories* 3, no. 2 (2019): 123–46. https://doi.org/10.1080/24701475.2019.1593667.

International Organization for Standardization. "Information and Documentation—Statistics and Quality Issues for Web Archiving." Geneva: International Organization for Standardization, 2013. https://www.iso.org/obp/ui/#iso:std:iso:tr:14873:ed-1:v1:en.

John, Nicholas A., and Asaf Nissenbaum. "An Agnotological Analysis of APIs: Or, Disconnectivity and the Ideological Limits of Our Knowledge of Social Media." *The Information Society* 35, no. 1 (January 2019): 1–12. https://doi.org/10.1080/01972243.2018.1542647.

Kilbride, William. "Making History: Digital Preservation and Electronic Legal Deposit in the Second Quarter of the 21st Century." In *Electronic Legal Deposit*, edited by Paul Gooding and Melissa Terras, 139–58. Facet, 2019. https://doi.org/10.29085/9781783303786.009.

Koehler, Wallace. "A Longitudinal Study of Web Pages Continued: A Consideration of Document Persistence." *Information Research* 9, no. 2 (2014). http://informationr.net/ir/9-2/paper174.html.

Koerbin, Paul. "Hit Save before Dot-Com Becomes Dot-Gone." *ABC News*, 8 May 2009. https://webarchive.nla.gov.au/awa/20180507173136/http://www.abc.net.au/news/2009-05-07/hit-save-before-dot-com-becomes-dot-gone/1674984.

Koerbin, Paul. "Revisiting the World Wide Web as Artefact: Case Studies in Archiving Small Data for the National Library of Australia's PANDORA Archive." In *Web 25: Histories from 25 Years of the World Wide Web*, edited by Niels Brügger, 191–206. Bern, Switzerland: Peter Lang, 2017.

Koerbin, Paul. "To Know, to Utter, to Argue … and to Archive and Access: What Place Does Archived Online Content Have in Social Media's Political Discourse? Part 2 of 2." *National Library of Australia Blog* (blog), 27 May 2014. https://webarchive.nla.gov.au/awa/20160719061925/https://www.nla.gov.au/blogs/web-archiving/2014/05/27/to-know-to-utter-to-argue-and-to-archive-and-access.

Krafft, Tobias D., Michael Gamer, and Katharina A. Zweig. "What Did You See? A Study to Measure Personalization in Google's Search Engine." *EPJ Data Science* 8, no. 1 (December 2019): 38. https://doi.org/10.1140/epjds/s13688-019-0217-5.

Legislative Services Branch. Library and Archives of Canada Act 2004 (2015). https://laws-lois.justice.gc.ca/eng/acts/l-7.7/.

Littman, Justin. "Twitter's Developer Policies for Researchers, Archivists, and Librarians." On *Archivy* (blog), 8 January 2019. https://medium.com/on-archivy/twitters-developer-policies-for-researchers-archivists-and-librarians-63e9ba0433b2.

Lomborg, Stine, and Anja Bechmann. "Using APIs for Data Collection on Social Media." *The Information Society* 30, no. 4 (8 August 2014): 256–65. https://doi.org/10.1080/01972243.2014.915276.

Major, Daniela, and Daniel Gomes. "Web Archives Preserve Our Digital Collective Memory." In *The Past Web: Exploring Web Archives*, edited by Daniel Gomes, Elena Demidova, Jane Winters, and Thomas Risse, 11–19. Cham: Springer, 2021. https://doi.org/10.1007/978-3-030-63291-5_2.

McCown, Frank, and Michael L. Nelson. "What Happens When Facebook Is Gone?" In Proceedings of the 2009 Joint International Conference on Digital Libraries - JCDL "09, 251–54. Austin, TX, USA: ACM Press, 2009. https://doi.org/10.1145/1555400.1555440.

Mehta, Ivan, and Manish Singh. "Twitter to End Free Access to Its API in Elon Musk's Latest Monetization Push." *TechCrunch* (blog), 2 February 2023. https://techcrunch.com/2023/02/01/twitter-to-end-free-access-to-its-api/.

National Library of Australia. "Menzies Collection." National Library of Australia, 2019. https://www.nla.gov.au/collections/guide-selected-collections/menzies-collection.

Nieborg, David, and Thomas Poell. "The Platformization of Cultural Production: Theorizing the Contingent Cultural Commodity." *New Media & Society* 20, no. 11 (2018): 4275–92. https://doi.org/10.1177/1461444818769694.

Nielsen, Rasmus Kleis, and Sarah Anne Ganter. *The Power of Platforms: Shaping Media and Society*. Oxford University Press, 2022.

Oguz, Fatih, and Wallace Koehler. "URL Decay at Year 20: A Research Note." *Journal of the Association for Information Science and Technology* 67, no. 2 (2016): 477–79. https://doi.org/10.1002/asi.23561.

Pennock, Maureen. "Web-Archiving." York, United Kingdom: Digital Preservation Coalition, 2013. https://citeseerx.ist.psu.edu/viewdoc/download?doi=10.1.1.384.5280&rep=rep1&type=pdf.

Plantin, Jean-Christophe, Carl Lagoze, Paul N Edwards, and Christian Sandvig. "Infrastructure Studies Meet Platform Studies in the Age of Google and Facebook." *New Media & Society* 20, no. 1 (2018): 293–310. https://doi.org/10.1177/1461444816661553.

Ramesh, Randeep, and Alex Hern. "Conservative Party Deletes Archive of Speeches from Internet." *The Guardian*, 13 November 2013. https://www.theguardian.com/politics/2013/nov/13/conservative-party-archive-speeches-internet.

Robinson, Helena. "Remembering Things Differently: Museums, Libraries and Archives as Memory Institutions and the Implications for Convergence." *Museum Management and Curatorship* 27, no. 4 (2012): 413–29. https://doi.org/10.1080/09647775.2012.720188.

Rogers, Richard. "Doing Web History with the Internet Archive: Screencast Documentaries." *Internet Histories* 1, no. 1–2 (2017): 160–72. https://doi.org/10.1080/24701475.2017.1307542.

Society of American Archivists. "Web Archives." Accessed 30 October 2023. https://dictionary.archivists.org/entry/web-archives.html.

State Library of New South Wales. "Digital Collecting Strategy." Sydney: State Library of New South Wales, 2014. https://www.sl.nsw.gov.au/sites/default/files/digital_collecting_strategy_version_1.0_-_8_december_2014.pdf.

Stokel-Walker, Chris. "Twitter's $42,000-per-Month API Prices Out Nearly Everyone." *Wired*, 10 March 2023. https://www.wired.com/story/twitter-data-api-prices-out-nearly-everyone/.

Thomson, Sara Day, and William Kilbride. "Preserving Social Media: The Problem of Access." *New Review of Information Networking* 20, no. 1–2 (2015): 261–75. https://doi.org/10.1080/13614576.2015.1114842.

Tromble, Rebekah. "Where Have All the Data Gone? A Critical Reflection on Academic Digital Research in the Post-API Age." *Social Media + Society* 7, no. 1 (2021). https://doi.org/10.1177/2056305121988929.

United Nations Educational, Scientific and Cultural Organisation. "Charter on the Preservation of Digital Heritage," 15 October 2003. http://portal.unesco.org/en/ev.php-URL_ID=17721&URL_DO=DO_TOPIC&URL_SECTION=201.html.

Vlist, Fernando N. van der, Anne Helmond, Marcus Burkhardt, and Tatjana Seitz. "API Governance: The Case of Facebook's Evolution." *Social Media + Society* 8, no. 2 (2022). https://doi.org/10.1177/20563051221086228.

Webster, Peter. "Users, Technologies, Organisations: Towards a Cultural History of World Web Archiving." In *Web 25: Histories from 25 Years of the World Wide Web*, edited by Niels Brügger, 179–90. Bern, Switzerland: Peter Lang, 2017.

Wikipedia contributors. "List of Web Archiving Initiatives." Wikipedia, 23 November 2023. https://en.wikipedia.org/w/index.php?title=List_of_Web_archiving_initiatives&oldid=1186031072.

The Closed-Loop
Academic Publication and the Data Surveillance Conundrum[1]

Jordan S. Sly and Joseph A. Koivisto

Introduction

In this chapter, we will identify some of the potential implications of the increasingly closed-loop and metrics-based models of academic publishing, student learning platforms, integrated library systems, and personnel management software packages being developed and sold by an increasingly small number of academic solutions companies. We aim to understand the potential danger stemming from the tight connections between the scholarship that is produced under these conditions, the perceived value of this scholarship in the market, and impacts on future research funding, student development, faculty positions, and more. We are uneasy, as we will discuss, by the ways in which this constricting pipeline and increasingly closed-loop pipeline may endanger our shared values of academic freedom, access, and a scholarly environment

---

1 This chapter is a modified and updated version of a paper we presented at the Charleston Conference in 2022. Our presentation copy was made available in the Charleston Conference Proceedings from that year, 2022, edited by Beth Bernhardt, Leah Hinds, and Lars Meyer, https://doi.org/10.3998/mpub.14369519. We are very appreciative to the editors who have given their permission for us to present our work in this present volume.

free from commercial influence in libraries and in higher education more broadly.[2] To our original assessment of these concerns, we have also added an analysis based on Nielsen and Ganter's *The Power of Platforms*—as others in this volume have done—and are using aspects of their framework to further address concerns we highlighted previously.[3] Additionally, we are working with Nielsen and Ganter's notion of an "information asymmetry" to wrestle with some of the complexities and similarities relating to the power of academic enterprise platforms as well as the media landscape and the power dynamics of new media described in their work.

For this chapter, the notion of an information asymmetry relates to the dynamic created and fostered by these companies, their increasingly opaque data practices which confound external inquiry and critique, and the reliance the higher education industry has on their products for multiple aspects of the research, funding, and administrative functions that we again define as a closed-loop pipeline with this asymmetry at its core. It is no mystery that large academic solutions companies like Clarivate/ProQuest, Elsevier, and others have the sole mission of profit. This fact is not controversial, but the question arises, to what extent does this mission undermine well-established objectives of higher education administration, teaching, and library services? As we will discuss below, there is some indication that these platforms are seeking the data-as-product models familiar in "Big Tech," but ignoring, or at least uncritically sidestepping the lessons learned through

---

2   For more on the ethical dilemmas of librarians in this framework see Andrew Weiss, "Libraries, Privacy, and Surveillance Capitalism: The Looming Trouble with Academia and Invasive Information Technologies," in Sarah Hartman-Caverly and Alexandria Chisholm (eds), *Practicing Privacy Literacy in Academic Libraries: Theories, Methods, and Cases*, (Chicago, IL: Association of College & Research Libraries, 2023).

3   Rasmus Kleis Nielsen and Sarah Anne Ganter, *The Power of Platforms: Shaping Media and Society. Oxford Studies in Digital Politics.* (Oxford, New York: Oxford University Press, 2022).

the major actors in that space. What is meant by this? If we think of large social media companies like Meta (owner of Facebook, Instagram, Threads, Whatsapp, and more) and X (formally Twitter), it is a now well-known Faustian bargain that in exchange for platforms we can use to connect to people we have given these companies our data which is then used for both market capture and penetration, advertisement placement pricing, and direct sales methods. By collecting, collating, and reselling our data, these companies found a lucrative new business model. There is some indication that academic enterprise platforms are following this path as we will show below.

Central to our concerns are a series of questions that are vital to consider in the coming years as these platforms continue to evolve and consolidate. First, we ask if the publications-as-data model of large publishing and educational technology platforms has created a closed-loop pipeline that endangers library values and university goals through the narrowing of impact-ratio focused research and the development of a surveillance publishing model that could dramatically impact the future of academic freedom for students, faculty, and libraries. To clarify, we are looking at the potential attenuation and narrowing of research areas based on the citation matrix and high-impact model for publisher reputation, vendor pricing, and library acquisitions and the lasting impact this may have on the research enterprise and student outcomes in which researchers (and perhaps more importantly university administrators) value publisher quantification and metrics over the traditional values of original scholarly output and a culture of iterative scholarly communications.

Second, if it can be said that universities have become both the data source and the consumer, whose hand is on the wheel determining what data is to be collected and sold and how it is used? Can the emphasis placed on return on investment (ROI) and research investments tip the scales to the point where there is a tangible narrowing of the research enterprise? Our second question looks at the notions of the data focus on publications and how this is being packaged and sold to universities. This is not just in the form of research databases, but also in the form of metrics counting for promotions and other human statistical purposes such as retention, recruitment, and research funding within the university. The question is threefold: 1) does the privileging of the citation information favor specific disciplines; 2) does this impact the research direction of the university, and whose hand is on the wheel with this privilege; and 3) are there customers outside of the university apparatus who benefit from this direction?

Third, what is the future of surveillance technology for controlling student and faculty behavior? As institutions—through their procurement decisions and in pursuit of systematic efficiency—integrate more and more vendor solutions into every stage of higher education administration and the research lifecycle, the data collection stream for major platform vendors and publishers further establishes a profit motive to participate in surveillance activities. What might possible outcomes be for our institutions, our researchers, and our students when commercial entities not only drive researcher behavior through metrics-based representation of scholarly import but also extract capital from the very audiences under the direct influence of their evaluative ideologies?

Fourth, are libraries forced to abandon ethical obligations due to the condensed marketplace for scholarly works? To what extent do the acquisitions and acceptance of these models clash with our professional ethics? Are we maintaining our goals as a profession or are we inadvertently helping to steer the direction of research to align with the needs of industries that may work against our collective ethics?

Finally, to what extent have we in higher education broadly, but also academic libraries more specifically, done this to ourselves? By volunteering our work into this quantified system and allowing, (to paraphrase Theodore Porter) metrics and assessment to make decisions without the imposition of needing to decide, in other words, to trust in the purity and objectivity of numbers, does this equate to ignoring the whole of the snake while it devours itself?[4]

The Problem for Higher Education

While there are political and ideological debates present in the external critiques of modern higher education, internally it has been discussed in opinion pieces in publications like *The Chronicle of Higher Education* (CHE), the *Times Higher Education* (THE), and within domain scholarly journals that one of the biggest risks to the longevity of higher education is the hyper-neoliberalization, commercialization, and quantification of the industry.[5] Authors arrive at this conclusion through

---

4 Theodore M. Porter, *Trust in Numbers: The Pursuit of Objectivity in Science and Public Life* (Princeton: Princeton University Press, 2020), 8.

5 For a few examples of this in *The Chronicle of Higher Education* please see Amna Khalid, "How Students are Furthering Academe's Corporatization by Insisting on Bureaucratic Solutions to Diversity Problems, they are Empowering Administrations at the Expense of the Faculty", CHE, May 4, 2021. ; Ryan Boyd, "The Syllabus Reads you: Our Pedagogies Cannot be Divorced from our Working Conditions", CHE, September 24, 2020. ; Daniel Bessner and Michael Brenes, "A Moral Stain on the Profession: As the Humanities Collapse, it is Time to Name and Shame the Culprits", CHE, April 26, 2019. ; Andrew Piper and Chad Wellmon, "How the Academic Elite Reproduces Itself", CHE, October 8, 2017. For some examples in the *Times Higher Education* please see, Jonathan R. Goodman, "Citation Counting is Killing Academic Dissent", THE, November 25, 2019.; Rebecca Natow and Kevin Dougherty, "Neoliberalism is not Always Negative, THE, March 21, 2019.; Vladimir Tismaneanu, "Neoliberalism Denounced", THE, September 18, 2014. For a small selection of the scholarly literature please see Beth Mintz, "Neoliberalism and the Crisis in Higher Education: The Cost of Ideology", *The American Journal of Economics and Sociology*, 80 (1), 2021.; Kevin J. Dougherty and Rebecca S. Natow, "Performance-Based Funding for Higher Education: How well does Neoliberal Theory Capture Neoliberal Practice?", *Higher Education*, 80, 2020. For additional books in this area see Stefan Collini, *What are Universities for?* (London: Penguin, 2012); Martha C. Nussbaum, *Not for Profit: Why Democracy Needs the Humanities* (Princeton: Princeton University Press 2016); Lawrence Busch, *Knowledge for Sale: The Neoliberal Takeover of Higher Education* (London: Penguin, 2017); Penny Jane Burke, "Gender, Neoliberalism, and Corporatized Higher Education," in Nancy S. Niemi and Marcus B. Weaver-Hightower, *The Wiley Handbook of Gender Equity in Higher Education* (Hoboken: Wiley, 2020); Mark Olssen, "Neoliberal Competition in Higher Education Today", in *A Normative Foucauldian* (Leiden: Brill, 2021).

various observations within their own subfields, but often extrapolate outwards towards the wider university community. A recent example of the critique of the focus on the numerical output or quantification of the research enterprise are the authors Elizabeth Chatterjee and Christopher Newfield who, in their respective chapters of *Limits of the Numerical*, outline the ways in which the recent focus on quantification has changed the ways we run our universities for the worse, especially as it pertains to the development and fostering of subject expertise.[6] As universities seek to find efficiencies to maximize entrepreneurial outputs and profit, education enterprise companies are more than willing to provide all the tools necessary for each stage of the academic pipeline, from personnel recruitment, development, and advancement to research creation, publication, and use.

To many, quantification is a way of measuring prestige as it determines selectivity both in the hiring of professors and the selection of students and creates an elite university setting. As Pierre Bourdieu showed in his ethnographic study *Homo Academicus*, however, this is not an evenly distributed sentiment as the hierarchies of academic power are not distributed to all areas of the university equally.[7] Central to Bourdieu's work is the notion of power, prestige, and privilege within the universities he studied. The book itself is highly contextualized by its time and location, but Bourdieu's insight into the constricting influence of academic power is relevant. Bourdieu notes that

---

[6] Elizabeth Chatterjee, "Numbers without Experts: The Populist Politics of Quantification," in *Limits of the Numerical: The Abuses and Uses of Quantification*, ed. Christopher Newfield, Anna Alexandrova, and Stephen John, (Chicago: University of Chicago Press, 2022), 23-46; Christopher Newfield "The Role of the Numerical in the Decline of Expertise,"in *Limits of the Numerical: The Abuses and Uses of Quantification*, ed. Christopher Newfield, Anna Alexandrova, and Stephen John, (Chicago: University of Chicago Press, 2022), 47-67.

[7] Pierre Bourdieu, *Homo Academicus*. Translated by Peter Collier, (Stanford: Stanford University Press, 1984).

the power of certain academics—by discipline, by impact, by status—has something of a stultifying effect on the development of research as the burden of this prestige hinders alternate work. Extrapolating this to today we can think about the use of tools like Web of Science which allow researchers to focus only on the most highly cited literature relevant to their field (despite valuable efforts to correct this pattern through targeted equity-focused literature and systematic reviews), which of course is a self-repeating cycle that privileges certain researchers, academic disciplines, universities, journals, and publishers more than others.[8]

What is significant here is the monetization of what can be paraphrased as a prestige-power cycle of the *Homo Academicus* both internally to the universities and to the external enterprise vendors. For a more current accounting of the concerns over quantification, Stefan Collini's work addresses the history and values of universities from the perspective of the internal industry concerns.[9] Importantly, Collini, like Bourdieu, looks at the cultures and structures of higher education and the threat of quantification on the scholarly apparatus. Collini picks up on Bourdieu's general notion of elite academic power, but further discusses the economic impact and incentive of universities to quantify and focus on the impact of particular disciplines over others. While the work ranges in its scope, it discusses the ways in which the business incentives of the modern university find purchase in the corporate sponsors on both ends of the prestige-power cycle discussed above.[10] This has impacts on both graduate job placement on the one end and research derived innovations on the other—sponsored and supported by interests outside of the university

---

8   Bourdieu, *Homo Academicus*.

9   Stefan Collini, *Speaking of Universities* (London: Verso, 2017).

10 Collini, *Speaking of Universities*.

itself. As Sun-Ha Hong discusses, the reliance on extracted data is self-consuming, cyclical, and reflects the input model on which the developing data cycle.[11] In other words, it creates and reinforces the world it reflects. Hong specifically discusses behavioral and punitive technology, but we argue that the same ideas of a reflective reliance model can be applied in the canonizing of academic work within the models being discussed by enterprise vendors. This model has the potential to create and foster disciplinary hegemonic parameters thereby hindering innovative research due to the reliance on a cyclical model for grant awards, citation, publications, graduate student thesis development, and much more. What we see is a shift in the nature of innovation along the lines of what Friedrich Engels feared, noting that "If society has a technical need, it serves as a greater spur to the progress of science than do ten universities...."[12] What Engels is developing is a progressive sense of innovation in which the needs of society both determine the nature and direction of innovation and create solutions outside of the realm of the expert or the genius. What we have witnessed through the development of these closed-loop systems, however, is an isolated and potentially artificial society of innovation separated from both the pure academic milieu and that of the more populous need.

This shift matters greatly in the world of higher education because quantification furthers the internal stratification of academic prestige, increases the reliance on large enterprise companies who can leverage this prestige, and furthers the interests of stakeholders outside of the industry. This situation is made potentially more dire with the innovations

---

11 Sun-Ha Hong, "Prediction as Extraction of Discretion," ACM Conference on Fairness, Accountability, and Transparency, June 2022. https://doi.org/10.1145/3531146.3533155.

12 Friedrich Engels, "Engels' Letter to Hans Starkenburg London, January 25, 1894," in *Towards the Understanding of Karl Marx: A Revolutionary Interpretation*, by Sidney Hook, 279–81, (New York: John Day Co., 1933).

in generative artificial intelligence (AI) and the discussions around AI-generated academic content pulling from this set of enshrined data and content we are describing. The shifts in the broader technology world, both in terms of advances in the social and semantic web and the increasingly dense interconnections with our everyday environments, demonstrate the speed and dominance these innovations hold over our existence in nearly every facet of our lives to both harmful and helpful ends. The substantial point in confronting this issue is to critique the accretion and the *de facto* nature of these shifts which privilege some groups over others by the inbuilt biases of the creators of this technology implicitly or explicitly.[13] The implications of data-driven societal engineering are not solely confined to the world of consumer technology, however. Critical literature exists inside of higher education technology literature, too, as Björn Brembs has written about algorithmic employment decisions in academia and the nature of the academic enterprise in the near-term and long-term futures. Most importantly, Brembs discusses the ways that the academic publisher Elsevier has shifted their business model away from publishing and towards data collection and analysis, thereby creating a market of internal and cyclical referential and quantified metrics creating the standards of success and throttling access to the means of attaining it.[14] Hiring is based on a set of determined metrics, in this model, and these metrics set the standard for impactful research, the quantification of productivity, and the return on investment both at an institutional level (in terms of hires and graduate projects) and at the funding level, when grant funding is involved.

---

13   Much of the framing of this section is a reflection of the work of Shoshana Zuboff and her work *The Age of Surveillance Capitalism*. Additionally, Safiya Umoja Noble's work *Algorithms of Oppression* is a critical introduction into the notions of implicit bias in the software and information systems development.

14   Björn Brembs, "Algorithmic Employment Decisions In Academia?" *björn.brembs.blog* (blog), September 23, 2021, https://bjoern.brembs.net/2021/09/algorithmic-employment-decisions-in-academia/.

This reliance on data creates a problem for higher education institutions who are competing for students, faculty, and research prestige, and companies like Clarivate or Elsevier can easily sell solutions to this problem. Increasingly, too, the competitiveness of a university within its own constricting marketplace due to the general global decline in the perception of universities as a worthwhile enterprise depends on these precise metrics being facilitated internally, yet levered externally.[15] As noted above, university administrators can turn to statistics and assessment metrics as a way of making decisions with a sense of rationality, despite the inbuilt biases of these numbers. It is critical to think about the automatic use of numbers as a deciding factor in any aspect of the research enterprise. As discussed above, the funding cycles for research vary based on the perceived importance of the research, often favoring the sciences, especially health sciences far more than other disciplines. Additionally, there is the nature of the research itself to contend with. Publication across academic areas, too, is vastly different and difficult if not impossible to compare directly. Therefore, *prima facie*, there is an inherent problem in the quantification of research. Additionally, as Chris Haufe has recently discussed, these disciples are put into false comparative modes which elide or erase the academic foundations and commonalities inherently based on shared philosophical and epistemological grounding.[16]

---

15 Collini, *Speaking of Universities*. Especially chapter 2 titled "Measuring Up: Universities and 'Accountability'" pp. 36-60.

16 Chris Haufe, in *Do the Humanities Create Knowledge*, (Cambridge: Cambridge University Press, 2023), investigates the philosophical origins of all human sciences and vital connective tissue that binds these studies. Valuable to recognize, of course, are the central ideas at the heart of a university and the foundations of a liberal education or artes liberales that fostered aspects of medieval scholasticism and the development of the European University as discussed in Charles H. Haskins' *The Rise of Universities*, (Ithaca: Cornell University Press 1957).

For universities, the harnessing of numbers allows for a clear expression of values through what or who is emphasized in the collected and assessed data. This is a general sociological trend, indicative of a value-set, an "ethics of numbers," focused on the "correctness" of data, as in its accuracy and the ways in which the data demonstrates a return on a specific investment or initiative as opposed to a desire to investigate its construction.[17] This affects both the institution's sense of its purpose and the researchers'; the numbers and the way they are assessed determine their value. For example, recent studies have found that the impact factor and prestige of a particular journal outweighed the value of the scholar themselves within a sample set of papers that they tracked.[18] This is important because, as Collini and others have shown, the rise in metrics and quantification has benefitted the publishing industry in an outsized way. The favoring of the journal as a method of citation analysis demonstrates that control over the publication, and availability of these journals is a way to ensure demand and profitability. From a university perspective, the striving for faculty to perform within these journals then becomes a metrics cycle of outlay, talent development, and research material procurement. Another outcome of the use of metrics is the gamification of the promotions and tenure processes and the process of applying for research funds and grants by emphasizing the role of bibliometrics as a pragmatic way of demonstrating researcher value above the noise of the academic publishing morass. As a result, however, researchers have found that the journal prestige and impact was

---

[17] Wendy Nelson Espeland and Michael Sauder, "Rankings and Reactivity: How Public Measures Recreate Social Worlds," *American Journal of Sociology* 113, no. 1 (2007): 1–10.; Porter, *Trust in Numbers*.

[18] Michael Callaham, Robert L. Wears, and Ellen Weber, "Journal Prestige, Publication Bias, and Other Characteristics Associated with Citation of Published Studies in Peer-Reviewed Journals," *Journal of the American Medical Association* 287, no. 21 (2002): 2847–50.

more valuable than the reputation of the researcher themselves in the overall citation index score.[19] There have even been studies to indicate that this citation emphasis on specific journals deemed high impact through Social Science Citation Index (SSCI) aggregation implies some evidence of citational bias; that by following the high impact citations scholars were unintentionally promulgating a strain of academic ideology that favored specific disciplinary interpretations and not others.[20] Again, this demonstrates some of the dangers in the winnowing out of research avenues in favor of prestige citation metrics and the appearance of academic favoritism. In a recent book, Sarah Lamdan has discussed the shared prestige games that are carried out in this metrics cycle and the ways in which this quantification shapes the research outlay as she notes the "monopolist" practices of certain publishers have facilitated a cycle wherein the journal becomes "…more important than the substance of their [the researchers'] work," adding that "in some cases, scholars feel obliged to tailor their work to journals that will raise their 'scholarly impact' numbers."[21] Put into short form, the values of a university reflect the revenue stream, and the metrics work towards a positive reaffirmation of this focus. In other words, the quantification of university values allows an abstraction that works to justify a particular set of needs of the university apparatus through the guise of routine assessment and rankings and enforces

---

19 Christopher R. Carpenter, David C. Cone, and Cathy C. Sarli, "Using Publication Metrics to Highlight Academic Productivity and Research Impact," *Academic Emergency Medicine* 2, no. 10 (2014): 1160–72.

20 Daniel B. Klein and Eric Chiang, "The Social Science Citation Index: A Black Box—with an Ideological Bias?" *Economics Journal Watch* 1, no. 1 (2004): 134–65.

21 Sarah Lamdan, *Data Cartels: The Companies That Control and Monopolize Our Information* (Palo Alto: Stanford University Press, 2022), 65. Lamdan's critique of these publishers and her description of them as monopolistic and "rent-seeking" can be found on p. 54.

a potentially stultifying hegemony and standardization that continues the funnel of academic power and prestige.

To many academic institutions and libraries, open access appears to be a valuable way of circumventing issues inherent in the quantification cycle. Open access scholars like Peter Suber have long discussed the issues of the monopolistic scholarly publishing industry and the publication conundrum of prestige, citation tracking, and impact, noting this as a significant obstacle blocking equitable publishing landscapes.[22] Increasingly, the inequalities and problems plaguing university research models have become more globally understood with research across disciplines demonstrating solidarity against arbitrary quantification and the extraordinarily high costs of research material. Additionally, as Posada and Chen discuss, the move to open access by many universities has caused the big publishers to seek additional sources of revenue and consolidate control and market share through mergers and acquisitions and by developing tools to ensure that customers are driven towards these products. Crucially, they also found that university strategies and research funding followed the metrics of high impact research provided and supported by these companies.[23] As Grossmann and Brembs discuss, the cost creep incurred by libraries reflects this pivot. Increasingly, the enterprise companies spend huge amounts on lobbying, technology, and direct-to-consumer initiatives, and additional contracts (government research, private research organizations, etc.) as well as researching and implementing differentiated costing models to ensure profit through off-set models

---

22 Much of this work, which can be found across many publications, is summarized in his 2012 *Open Access*.

23 Alejandro Posada and George Chen, *Inequality in Knowledge Production: The Integration of Academic Infrastructure by Big Publishers* (Toronto: HAL Open Science ELPUB, 2018).

that shift payments from the back-end to the front-end of the research cycle.[24]

The Problem for Academic Libraries

These companies understand the shifting nature of the academic landscape and the emphasis for an increased use of dynamic metrics. It is perhaps due to this increasing awareness that larger publishers are seeking new models. For example, Elsevier has established a more direct-to-consumer model connected to its Mendeley citation management platform. In fact, in her 2019 plenary presentation to the attendees of the Charleston Conference, Elsevier CEO Kumsal Bayazit discussed the importance of this method to facilitate cutting-edge research as universities and libraries sought negotiations, such as the successful negotiations of the California State University system, to increase access and publishing opportunities with Elsevier.[25] Additionally, the acquisition of ProQuest by Clarivate diversifies the reach of university enterprise needs, and platforms, like EBSCO's Panorama, provide active use metrics and impact data in conjunction with traditional research; furthermore, these factors along with companies like ProctorU control the educational experience of students, all combine to facilitate the full-scale quantification of higher education from students, to teaching, to research, to publication, and to hiring within a closed and metered loop.

The power of these academic enterprise management systems to control both the visibility of published material through metrics-derived and proprietary algorithmic weighting and

---

24 Alexander Grossmann and Björn Brembs, "Current Market Rates for Scholarly Publishing Services," *F1000 Research* 10, no. 20 (2021): 1–25.

25 Kumsal Bayazit and Cris Ferguson, "Collaborating to Support the Research Community, the Next Chapter," in *The Proceedings of the Charleston Conference*. Charleston, SC: Perdue, 2019. https://docs.lib.purdue.edu/charleston/2019/plenarysessions/1/.

to derive, store, and sell the back-end data associated with the creation and use of these materials creates an complementary (but not fully analogous) form of "information asymmetry" described by Rasmus Kleis Nielsen and Sarah Anne Ganter in their work *The Power of Platforms*, much discussed in this volume. As Nielsen and Ganter describe it, an information asymmetry is an expression of power of the platform over the user due to is ability to determine the rules and "...operate as opaque black boxes where outsiders only see input and output on the basis of limited and biased data; only the platforms are privy to how the processes work and have access to much more detailed data."[26] Within the context of this chapter, we are isolating for this chapter, the enterprise platforms in question can meter access to the data on which the higher education industry has become reliant on, creating an asymmetrical power dynamic. In Nielsen and Ganter, they investigate these power dynamics within the context of traditional media and social media platforms like Facebook and Twitter, but we argue that much of the same asymmetries exist in the academic context. Nielsen and Ganter's framework of what constitutes the power that a platform can exert by its instantiated and asserted presence can be paraphrased and simplified into the following basic ideas: platforms set the standards by which other operate, have the ability to make or break connections, automate action at scale, foster information asymmetries, and can operate across domains.[27] Data in the form of scholarship and scholar metrics (e.g. citation counts, grant information, and co-author networks) has been understood within a Foucauldian framework, to be a power over others as a form of dominion. The power to utilize this information

---

26 Nielsen and Ganter, *Power*, 21.

27 Nielsen and Ganter, *Power*, 21.; Rasmus Kleis Nielsen and Sarah Anne Ganter, "Dealing with Digital Intermediaries: A Case Study of the Relations Between Publishers and Platforms," *New Media & Society* 20, no. 4 (2017): 157-158.

hegemony fosters a closed-loop academic information economy with a central asymmetry akin to that described by Neilsen and Ganter in their definition of platforms and their power in the wider information economy. What is most concerning is the seemingly practiced naivety in these moves ignoring the lessons learned from social media sectors about the negative effects of this form of data usage and looking only at the revenue potential in reselling user data either externally or back to the end consumer.

Where do we, as libraries and librarians, find ourselves in this evolving environment of scholarly datafication and the production/consumption cycle of data-driven impact? Consider Jeff Pooley's 2022 article: in light of ProQuest's acquisition by Clarivate, Pooley presents surveillance publishing as a descriptor for companies that derive revenue by peddling predictive solutions to research questions based on aggregation and analysis of researcher behaviors. Be it searching for and accessing publications, research creation and publication, or citation, surveillance publishers are incentivized to bring insights to market that have been derived through user behavior tracking, distant machine-driven reading of the scholarly corpus, and impact metrics, all of which are aggregated and churned through the alchemical cauldron of trade-secret-protected analytical processes and algorithms. Or as Pooley puts it, "minting money from behavioral by-products."[28]

This methodology brings with it the numerous attendant issues of ceding control of scholarly communications and material evaluation to black box systems. Inherent bias and algorithmic racism, sexism, etc. enter a self-amplifying feedback cycle in which corporate-sourced assessments infect every corner of scholarly practice: hiring, promotion & tenure, grants,

---

28 Jefferson Pooley, "Surveillance Publishing," *Elephant in the Lab*, March 25, 2022, https://doi.org/10.5281/zenodo.6384605.

citation, and ultimately publication. Such datafication and the insights made thereof are not objective measures despite our collective habit of reflexively viewing quantitative and algorithm-based methods beyond the messiness of subjective, human insights. Sarah Lamdan observes that the "score-powered" system dependent on vendor-sourced metrics does little to repair racist and misogynistic legacies in the academy but rather turns them into data points, all the while establishing a scholarly environment the incentivizes greater accumulation of the academic literature in the pursuit of high-impact journal publication.[29] Furthermore, Dougherty, Nguyen, and Illingworth conclude that the relationships between scholarly quality of scientific journal articles and citation counts is inconsistent at best and, at worst, biased and misleading.[30] When we buy into these evaluative and infrastructural systems, we become complicit in the creation of an academic world in which up-and-coming researchers are incentivized to perform in ways that align with the corporate algorithmic interpretive lens rather than with the traditional academic values of scholarly rigor and societal impact. Throughout this process, we help to perpetuate this cycle by pumping the system full of more and more of its vital life sources: products to datafy and peddle (in the form of publications) and finance (in the form of subscription and license fees). We, the academy, have become the product *and* the consumer, all in one.

With the acquisition of ProQuest, Clarivate not only acquired a considerable cache of content, but they also obtained the corporate keys to library infrastructure through Ex Libris, one of the major producers of integrated library software. Now

---

29 Lamdan, *Data Cartels*, 63-65.

30 Michael R. Dougherty, Rosalind Nguyen, and David Illingworth, "A Memory-Theoretic Account of Citation Propagation," *PsyArXiv*, September 16, 2019, https://doi.org/10.31234/osf.io/zst69.

under the Clarivate corporate tent, library systems represent yet another data point to be fed into the scholarly insights machine. Additionally, and perhaps more alarmingly, libraries, at least through their software, have now become an additional module of monolithic corporate offerings for higher education software solutions. Through centralization and integration of libraries into a single suite of tools offering full coverage for university needs—enterprise management, library services, faculty performance tracking, tuition and fees management—claims of efficiency and seamless integration can be realized. But what for us would appear to be a seamless user experience is, for Clarivate, a seamless data collection activity.

Jamie Taylor addresses this notion in her piece "Mergers, Acquisitions, and My Tinfoil Hat," where she explains that while anxiety about these mergers may seem like the hand wringing of skeptics and contrarians, there is simply too much money to be made. Library systems themselves do not represent a growth market, and publishers have essentially pushed library collection budgets past the breaking point with subscription fees. Now, with the inclusion of libraries in the corporate holdings of academic insight firms, there appears to be yet another piece of the carcass to be used.[31]

Of course, this represents an ethical concern regarding patron privacy and extractive capitalist approaches towards user data. Because we already know library vendors collect, aggregate, reuse, and sell our data and data-derived insights, this is not a fanciful hypothetical. Now, we are faced with a reality in which data extraction and capitalization are not only lucrative, but also convenient. The convenience is only furthered by the almost universal transition of library software

---

31 Jamie Taylor, "Mergers, Acquisitions, and My Tinfoil Hat," *Librarian Shipwreck* (blog), 2021, https://librarianshipwreck.wordpress.com/2021/08/16/mergers-acquisitions-and-my-tinfoil-hat/.

to vendor-hosted software as a service (SaaS) models in which libraries use systems on servers that are beyond our control and scrutiny. Aside from vendor disclosures and assurances, we will not know what data they are collecting and how. But we will know that the collection process will be one step less complicated as the data already lives on their machines.

In fact, a 2022 disclosure from EBSCO to customers of the EBSCO Discovery platform revealed that a certain subset of user data was being collected unbeknownst to the users and their libraries. Collected data included search data and user clicks, which do not represent shocking data collection practices on the face of it. However, one affected institution took umbrage with the fact that EBSCO did not appear to realize that the data were being collected and that the institution had been given "dangerously incorrect information from them about what kind of data they currently collect".[32] Assurances were made that this data was not used for marketing purposes or supplied to law enforcement agencies. Rather, what is most illustrative about this incident is not that the data were collected, but the ease with which the collection occurred: seamlessly, without notification of institution or user, and seemingly by accident.

With the high likelihood of library data entering the academic counting machine, we are faced with the probability that our data will help to further the metrics-driven amplification cycle we have discussed. This is not a new prospect for libraries as bibliometrics and citation counts are frequently touted as objective levels of scholarly value. However, this new methodology is a sleeker, more efficient machine that integrates our data without us even lifting a finger.

And while we have harped heavily on Clarivate, they do not stand alone in this new environment. In 2022, Elsevier closed

---

32 The institution has asked to not be identified in this chapter.

their acquisition of Interfolio, a company that sells a variety of products that cover faculty searches and hires, promotion and tenure dossiers, faculty activity reporting, and more. Lamdan notes that Elsevier has made such extensive inroads into all functions of the academy—from recruitment to publication to promotion and tenure—"that it would be hard to separate universities from Elsevier's products and contracts".[33] Roger Schonfeld observes Elsevier's move is in direct competition with Clarivate, evincing a tit-for-tat corporate arms race whose measures of escalation will be who has the bigger data sets to analyze.[34] There is too much money to be made for companies not to explore every possible revenue stream.

Schonfeld also notes resistance to these types of mergers, stating that this must lead us to consider the implications of buying into one-stop-shop research infrastructure that bundles all of our data handling into a single pair of corporate hands.[35] This, in turn, raises the concern of vendor lock-in or, as Hamilton, Daniels, Smith, and Eaton prefer, "university captivity".[36] As more and more key institutional infrastructures are coupled into a monolithic service provider, the barrier to transition to an off-suite platform coerces libraries into making decisions based on the inertial pull of the metaphorical company store rather than our organizational needs and professional ethics. This captivity does not limit its negative impacts just to the coercive forces exerted on libraries; it creates

---

33 Lamdan, *Data Cartels*, 66.

34 Roger Schonfeld, "Elsevier Acquiring Interfolio," *The Scholarly Kitchen* (blog), April 25, 2022, https://scholarlykitchen.sspnet.org/2022/04/25/elsevier-acquire-interfolio/.

35 Roger Schonfeld, "Clarivate to Acquire Proquest," *The Scholarly Kitchen* (blog), May 18, 2021, https://scholarlykitchen.sspnet.org/2021/05/18/clarivate-to-acquire-proquest/.

36 Laura T. Hamilton, Heather Daniels, Christian Michael Smith, and Charlie Eaton, "The Private Side of Public Universities: Third-Party Providers and Platform Capitalism," UC Berkeley Center for Studies in *Higher Education Research & Occasional Papers Series* 3 (2022): 1–35.

a precedent for obscured data practices as the norm for university-vendor relationships. Expanding on Frank Pasquale's work in *Black Box Societies*, Tressie McMillan Cottom cautions that such vertically integrated SaaS approaches to service provision, especially in the academy, create a norm of administrative opacity that enables private data worlds that can evade democratic inquiry while ratcheting up extractive practices.[37] Our institutions underwrite this extraction in the name of cost-savings and efficiency. And we are fed the by-products of the system that we cannot evaluate, or likely escape, which then drive researcher and library behavior as well as profits.

Recent advances in AI only further complicate the matter as Clarivate, Elsevier, and others of their kind are well-positioned to benefit doubly from the inclusion of AI methodologies in their workflows and evaluative frameworks as they can streamline their workflows and feed user data into their models. In late 2023, Elsevier announced that they are offering datasets—including full-text articles, author profiles, citations, biomedical records, and chemical patents across 24 disciplines—as a product to train AI-enabled methodologies at the "vanguard of data science".[38] In light of the well-established pattern of material accumulation and hoarding, the winnowing of the vendor ecosystem, and the integration of vendor platforms into all functional areas of academia, the advent of AI-empowered research and evaluative methodologies creates yet another revenue stream for these corporations as long as they can find willing participants to supply them with

---

37 Tressie McMillan Cottom, "Where Platform Capitalism and Racial Capitalism Meet: The Sociology of Race and Racism in the Digital Society," *Sociology of Race and Ethnicity* 6, no. 4 (2020): 441–449.

38 Elsevier, "Elsevier Introduces Authoritative Scientific Datasets to Fuel Innovation and Business-Critical Decisions in Life Sciences, Chemicals and Other Research-Intensive Industries," Commercial website, elsevier.com, August 11, 2023. https://www.elsevier.com/about/press-releases/elsevier-introduces-authoritative-scientific-datasets-to-fuel-innovation-and.

data and revenue.[39] Institutions, it seems, are ready, willing, and able to welcome these new vendor offerings as a means of accelerating research production and automating away the repetitive, difficult aspects of administering academic enterprises. We have already seen calls for the integration of AI into student recruitment and admissions, peer review, and library operations.[40] While the prospect of outsourcing challenging and resource-intensive activities to these AI-enabled automation tools may seem attractive, it is incumbent on those of us in academia—administrators, instructors, researchers, librarians, and beyond—to think critically about what is sacrificed in the name of efficiency and expediency. The datafication necessary to enable these large AI models may further codify the entrenched biases present in scholarly practice while doing so at a speed and scale that was previously unimaginable and with the protective guise of objectivity assumed in "human-free" computational frameworks. Furthermore, support of these tools through both data and dollars only serves to increase vendor entanglement, making it increasingly impossible to separate our data and decisions from the omnipresent vendor profit motive.

In her 2021 book *A City is Not a Computer: Other Urban Intelligences*, Shannon Mattern reminds us that "Procurement is

---

39 See for example, Todd A. Carpenter, "AI Will Lead Us to Need More Garbage-Subtraction," *The Scholarly Kitchen* (blog), February 11, 2023, https://scholarlykitchen.sspnet.org/2023/11/02/we-need-more-garbage-subtraction-because-of-ai/.

40 See Rick Clark, "The End of 'Reading Season': AI Will Free the Admissions Staff from the Drudgery of Poring over Applications," *The Chronicle of Higher Education*, May 25, 2023, online edition, sec. The Review|Forum. https://www.chronicle.com/article/how-will-artificial-intelligence-change-higher-ed.; Haseeb Irfanullah, "Ending Human-Dependent Peer Review," *The Scholarly Kitchen* (blog), October 29, 2023, https://scholarlykitchen.sspnet.org/2023/09/29/ending-human-dependent-peer-review/.;, Hannah Herrlich, "The Future of Libraries: AI and Machine Learning," *Fordham Library News* (blog), May 23, 2023. https://librarynews.blog.fordham.edu/2023/05/23/the-future-of-libraries-ai-and-machine-learning/.

political—both in the police department and the library."[41] As every aspect of higher education, from the library to faculty activity tracking to promotion and tenure to research to impact assessment, becomes the target of techno-solutionist ideals of data connectedness and efficiency, we must consider the ethical and political implications of the technologies that we underwrite through our data and our dollars (in the case of public universities, public tax dollars). Our dollars and data no longer exist within a silo of library-centric needs and uses, but rather help to feed the larger insight machine that can have deleterious effects on scholarly behavior. As institutional data is conveniently and efficiently collected through vendor surveillance and fed back to the institution, at a hefty premium, we as librarians, through our procurement decisions, are implicated for our contributions. These metrics and insights shape behavior and demand, leading us to acquire journals because of impact, because they get cited the most, because they have the most impactful articles, because they court the most prestigious research, because their insights indicate what are the most impactful areas of scholarship, because we bought the most impactful journals, and so on and so on. As the trend towards vertical integration of ILS vendors, publishers, activity trackers, and enterprise management solutions, the impulse to chase visibility within these vendor-supplied models becomes less of a pursuit of efficiency and more of an echo chamber whose reach is comprehensive within the academic landscape, one that we are subsidizing with our data and our money.

---

41 Shannon Mattern, *A City Is Not a Computer: Other Urban Intelligences.* (Princeton: Princeton University Press, 2021), 84.

Conclusions

What can we make of this ever-evolving issue? On the one-hand, from the perspective of libraries, we must refrain from conspiratorial thinking. It is not surprising or controversial that for-profit enterprise, database, and academic platform companies are seeking to turn a profit. We should remain vigilant, however, of our, that is academia's, willingness to find the easy and convenient solution uncritically or without considering the longer-term effects of what they are selling. As we have illustrated here, there are many lessons to be learned from the tech world as they have dealt with many of these issues, and technologists and philosophers have spilled much ink thinking through the near-term and long-term ramifications of these issues. We can look internally, too, at our own recent history in academia to forecast the imminent impacts of an industry whose sole purpose is to profit from our output by repackaging and reselling our own products. We've seen in academia the increasing blind reliance on data and quantified metrics to inform all aspects of the university enterprise from research to personnel management to hiring—all of which is reliant on a feedback loop pre-determined by expectations set and reinforced through the products chosen to make these elements easier to assess. In a recent industry platform webinar we attended, academic enterprise representatives discussed the "alchemy" of user-derived data and their ability to repackage and sell this data, with consent, to software development companies with their key takeaway being a driver towards increased revenue. More to the point, they had learned the lessons of the tech industry, and more specifically the social media companies in understanding the data we generate can be used to target us, to sell to us, and to use us for further development. They discussed the ways in which the use of this data would become, like social media, intelligent and drive user behavior, further cinching the knot on the closed-loop as algorithmically-based suggestions further limit and constrain research and reinforce a status-quo enabled and enfranchised by profit motive in the guise of engagement, use, and reuse. Our collective buy-in to these platforms demonstrates our complacency towards these ideas—that, for sake of ease and assessment we in academia are willing to create and utilize a closed-loop system in which our research, our personnel management, our funding opportunities, our university strategic goals and initiatives, and more are constrained and contained—or trapped—within.

Bibliography

Bayazit, Kumsal, and Cris Ferguson. "Collaborating to Support the Research Community, the Next Chapter." In *The Proceedings of the Charleston Conference.* Charleston, SC: Perdue, 2019. https://docs.lib.purdue.edu/charleston/2019/plenarysessions/1/.

Bessner, Daniel, and Michael Brenes. "A Moral Stain on the Profession: As the Humanities Collapse, It Is Time to Name and Shame the Culprits." *Chronicle of Higher Education*, 26 April 2019.

Bourdieu, Pierre. *Homo Academicus*. Translated by Peter Collier. Stanford: Stanford University Press, 1984.

Boyd, Ryan. "The Syllabus Reads You: Our Pedagogies Cannot Be Divorced from Our Working Conditions." *Chronicle of Higher Education*, 24 September 2020.

Brembs, Björn. "Algorithmic Employment Decisions In Academia?" Björn.Brembs.Blog (blog), September 23, 2021. https://bjoern.brembs.net/2021/09/algorithmic-employment-decisions-in-academia/.

Burke, Penny Jane. "Gender, Neoliberalism, and Corporatized Higher Education." In *The Wiley Handbook of Gender Equity in Higher Education*, edited by Nancy S. Niemi and Marcus B. Weaver-Hightower. Hoboken: Wiley, 2020.

Busch, Lawrence. *Knowledge for Sale: The Neoliberal Takeover of Higher Education*. London: Penguin, 2017.

Callaham, Michael, Robert L. Wears, and Ellen Weber. "Journal Prestige, Publication Bias, and Other Characteristics Associated with Citation of Published Studies in Peer-Reviewed Journals." *Journal of the American Medical Association* 287, no. 21 (2002): 2847–50.

Carpenter, Christopher R., David C. Cone, and Cathy C. Sarli. "Using Publication Metrics to Highlight Academic Productivity and Research Impact." *Academic Emergency Medicine* 2, no. 10 (2014): 1160–72.

Carpenter, Todd A. "AI Will Lead Us to Need More Garbage-Subtraction." *The Scholarly Kitchen* (blog), February 11, 2023. https://scholarlykitchen.sspnet.org/2023/11/02/we-need-more-garbage-subtraction-because-of-ai/.

Chatterjee, Elizabeth. "Numbers without Experts: The Populist Politics of Quantification." In *Limits of the Numerical: The Abuses and Uses of Quantification*, edited by Christopher Newfield, Anna Alexandrova, and Stephen John, 23–46. Chicago: University of Chicago Press, 2022.

Clark, Rick. "The End of 'Reading Season': AI Will Free the Admissions Staff from the Drudgery of Poring over Applications." *Chronicle of Higher Education*, May 25, 2023, online edition, sec. The Review|Forum. https://www.chronicle.com/article/how-will-artificial-intelligence-change-higher-ed.

Collini, Stefan. *What Are Universities For?* London: Penguin, 2012.

Collini, Stefan. *Speaking of Universities*. London: Verso, 2017.

Cottom, Tressie McMillan. "Where Platform Capitalism and Racial Capitalism Meet: The Sociology of Race and Racism in the Digital Society." *Sociology of Race and Ethnicity* 6, no. 4 (2020): 441–49.

Dougherty, Kevin, and Rebecca Natow. "Performance-Based Funding for Higher Education: How Well Does Neoliberal Theory Capture Neoliberal Practice?" *Higher Education* 80 (2020).

Dougherty, Michael R., Rosalind Nguyen, and David Illingworth. "A Memory-Theoretic Account of Citation Propagation." *PsyArXiv*, September 16, 2019. https://doi.org/10.31234/osf.io/zst69.

Elsevier. "Elsevier Introduces Authoritative Scientific Datasets to Fuel Innovation and Business-Critical Decisions in Life Sciences, Chemicals and Other Research-Intensive Industries." Commerical website. elsevier.com, August 11, 2023. https://www.elsevier.com/about/press-releases/elsevier-introduces-authoritative-scientific-datasets-to-fuel-innovation-and.

Engels, Friedrich. "Engels' Letter to Hans Starkenburg London, January 25, 1894." In *Towards the Understanding of Karl Marx: A Revolutionary Interpretation*, by Sidney Hook, 279–81. New York: John Day Co., 1933.

Espeland, Wendy Nelson, and Michael Sauder. "Rankings and Reactivity: How Public Measures Recreate Social Worlds." *American Journal of Sociology* 113, no. 1 (2007): 1–10.

Goodman, Jonathan R. "Citation Counting Is Killing Academic Dissent." *Times Higher Education*, 25 November 2019.

Grossmann, Alexander, and Björn Brembs. "Current Market Rates for Scholarly Publishing Services." *F1000 Research* 10, no. 20 (2021): 1–25.

Hamilton, Laura T., Heather Daniels, Christian Michael Smith, and Charlie Eaton. "The Private Side of Public Universities: Third-Party Providers and Platform Capitalism." *UC Berkeley Center for Studies in Higher Education Research & Occasional Papers Series* 3 (2022): 1–35.

Haskins, Charles H. *The Rise of Universities*. Ithaca: Cornell University Press, 1957.

Haufe, Chris. *Do the Humanities Create Knowledge?* Cambridge: Cambridge University Press, 2024.

Herrlich, Hannah. "The Future of Libraries: AI and Machine Learning." *Fordham Library News* (blog), May 23, 2023. https://librarynews.blog.fordham.edu/2023/05/23/the-future-of-libraries-ai-and-machine-learning/.

Irfanullah, Haseeb. "Ending Human-Dependent Peer Review." *The Scholarly Kitchen* (blog), October 29, 2023. https://scholarlykitchen.sspnet.org/2023/09/29/ending-human-dependent-peer-review/.

Khalid, Amna. "How Students Are Furthering Academe's Corporatization by Insisting on Bureaucratic Solutions to Diversity Problems, They Are Empowering Administrations at the Expense of the Faculty." *The Chronicle of Higher Education*, 24 September 2020.

Klein, Daniel B., and Eric Chiang. "The Social Science Citation Index: A Black Box—with an Ideological Bias?" *Economics Journal Watch* 1, no. 1 (2004): 134–65.

Lamdan, Sarah. *Data Cartels: The Companies That Control and Monopolize Our Information*. Palo Alto: Stanford University Press, 2022.

Mattern, Shannon. *A City Is Not a Computer: Other Urban Intelligences*. Princeton: Princeton University Press, 2021.

Mintz, Beth. "Neoliberalism and the Crisis in Higher Education: The Cost of Ideology." *The American Journal of Economics and Sociology* 80, no. 1 (2021).

Newfield, Christopher. "The Role of the Numerical in the Decline of Expertise." In *Limits of the Numerical: The Abuses and Uses of Quantification*, edited by Christopher Newfield, Anna Alexandrova, and Stephen John, 47–67. Chicago: University of Chicago Press, 2022.

Natow, Rebecca, and Kevin Dougherty. "Neoliberalism Is Not Always Negative." *Times Higher Education*, 21 March 2019.

Nielsen, Rasmus Kleis, and Sarah Anne Ganter. "Dealing with Digital Intermediaries: A Case Study of the Relations Between Publishers and Platforms." *New Media & Society* 20, no. 4 (2017): 1600–1617.

Nielsen, Rasmus Kleis and Sarah Anne Ganter. *The Power of Platforms: Shaping Media and Society*. Oxford Studies in Digital Politics. (Oxford, New York: Oxford University Press, 2022).

Nussbaum, Martha C. *Not for Profit: Why Democracy Needs the Humanities*. Princeton: Princeton University Press, 2016.

Noble, Safiya Umoja. *Algorithms of Oppression: How Search Engines Reinforce Racism*. New York: NYU Press, 2018.

Olssen, Mark. "Neoliberal Competition in Higher Education Today". In *A Normative Foucauldian*. Leiden: Brill, 2021.

Piper, Andrew, and Chad Wellmon. "How the Academic Elite Reproduces Itself." *The Chronicle of Higher Education*, 8 October 2017.

Pooley, Jefferson. "Surveillance Publishing." *Elephant in the Lab*, n.d. https://doi.org/10.5281/zenodo.6384605.

Porter, Theodore M. *Trust in Numbers: The Pursuit of Objectivity in Science and Public Life*. Princeton: Princeton University Press, 2020.

Posada, Alejandro, and George Chen. *Inequality in Knowledge Production: The Integration of Academic Infrastructure by Big Publishers*. Toronto: HAL Open Science ELPUB, 2018.

Schonfeld, Roger. "Clarivate to Acquire Proquest." *The Scholarly Kitchen* (blog), May 18, 2021. https://scholarlykitchen.sspnet.org/2021/05/18/clarivate-to-acquire-proquest/.

Schonfeld, Roger. "Elsevier Acquiring Interfolio." *The Scholarly Kitchen* (blog), April 25, 2022. https://scholarlykitchen.sspnet.org/2022/04/25/elsevier-acquire-interfolio/.

Suber, Peter. *Open Access*. Cambridge: MIT Press, 2012.

Hong, Sun-Ha. "Prediction as Extraction of Discretion." ACM Conference on Fairness, Accountability, and Transparency, June 2022. https://doi.org/10.1145/3531146.3533155.

Taylor, Jamie. "Mergers, Acquisitions, and My Tinfoil Hat." *Librarian Shipwreck* (blog), 2021. https://wp.me/p38S12-JZ.

Tismaneanu, Vladimir. "Neoliberalism Denounced." *Times Higher Education*, 18 September 2014.

Weiss, Andrew. "Libraries, Privacy, and Surveillance Capitalism: The Looming Trouble with Academia and Invasive Information Technologies." in *Practicing Privacy Literacy in Academic Libraries: Theories, Methods, and Cases*, edited by Sarah Hartman-Caverly and Alexandria Chisholm, Chicago, IL: Association of College & Research Libraries, 2023.

Zuboff, Shoshana. *The Age of Surveillance Capitalism: The Fight for a Human Future at the New Frontier of Power*. New York: PublicAffairs, 2019.

Biographies

Christine F. Smith is an Associate Librarian and the Head of Acquisitions and Serials at Concordia University Library in Montreal, Quebec, Canada. Passionate about the study and facilitation of connection to information, Smith takes an interdisciplinary approach in researching systems and structures—both technologically and socially constructed—that accelerate and impede the sharing of knowledge.

Elena Rowan is completing her Master of Arts in Sociology at Concordia University. Her current research explores library advocacy around ebook licensing. She is a research assistant at Concordia's Data Justice Hub, looking at how activists gather and make sense of data.

lisa Hooper is Head of Media Services at Tulane University. In this role, she works to provide equitable opportunities for interdisciplinary discovery, innovative scholarship, and skill development through creative play with multimedia collections and media tools. This work includes providing access through purchasing and licensing a wide array of film content for pedagogical and research purposes across the disciplines.

Dr. Kieran Hegarty is a librarian and sociologist. He is currently a Research Fellow in Media & Communication at RMIT University. Kieran's work examines how public institutions, infrastructures and values are evolving in an era of digital and social media. His PhD research examined how online material is incorporated into major public library collections, and the effects that a changing information environment has on the public's right to access and contribute to the shared cultural record. Kieran has published on critical histories of library standards, the impact of platform power on web archiving, and the history and politics of knowledge production about libraries in a range of media and information studies journals, including *Information, Communication & Society, Internet Histories, New Media & Society* and *Journal of Critical Library and Information Studies.*

Jordan S. Sly (jsly@umd.edu) is a historian of early modern European intellectual and cultural history, instructor of library and information science, and serves as the Head of the Humanities and Social Science Librarians at the University of Maryland. His historical research focuses on the interplay between knowledge, information dissemination, and cultural development during the early modern period, often examining how libraries, archives, and other repositories of knowledge influenced society and intellectual life. This background informs his interdisciplinary approach, connecting historical insights with contemporary issues in information science and digital humanities such as the evolving roles of libraries, information ethics, and the digital transformation of research practices.

Joseph A. Koivisto (jkoivist@umd.edu) is the Head of Consortial Digital Initiatives for the USMAI Library Consortium, headquartered at the University of Maryland. His work centers on library system administration and support, development of custom software solutions for library platforms and data, and open access distribution of scholarly works. His research focuses on library software and data management, open library platforms, and controlled vocabularies.

Index

academic film streaming platforms.
See also commercial film streaming platforms; streaming film platforms
  distribution models, 66–67, 73–75
  library collections impact, 70–71, 73–74, 80–81
  licensing over ownership structure, 73, 75, 80–81
  market capture, 69–70
academic publishing platforms. *See* closed-loop academic publishing
Alexander, Neta, 78
Alexander Street Press, 69
AlgorithmWatch, 108
Allison-Cassin, Stacy, 11–12
Amazon, 71–72
Appleton, Leo, 14
Arnold, Sarah, 76–77
artificial intelligence (AI), 123, 135–136
audiobooks. *See* digital lending platforms
Australian Search Experience, 108

Bannerman, Sara, 10
Bayazit, Kumsal, 128
Ben-David, Anat, 106
Berman, Sandy, 12
bias
  in academic publishing, 130–131, 136
  diversity decreased in platforms, 15–16
  in library structures, 12
  in platforms' metadata, 12–13
Blackwell, Michael, 41–42, 45, 52–54
Blomley, Nick, 33
Bourdieu, Pierre, 120–121
Breeding, Marshall, 7, 13
Brembs, Björn, 123, 127

Cambridge Analytica, 92, 104
Canadian Urban Libraries Council, 50
capitalism. *See also* licensing; market capture
  business models, 38–39, 42, 128
  foundations of platform power, 1
  information as commodity, 6, 16–17
  platforms and libraries, overview, 6–8
  profit incentives of platforms, 7, 39–40, 53, 77–78, 90, 116, 118, 127–128, 136
  technology of platforms and, 2–3
censorship, 47
Chatterjee, Elizabeth, 120
Chen, George, 127
Clarivate, 69, 124, 128, 130, 131–132, 134
closed-loop academic publishing, 129–130. *See also* digital lending platforms; higher education
  artificial intelligence (AI) and, 135–136
  author's overview, 115–119
  complacency towards, 138–139
  cost for libraries, 127–128, 132
  data as product, 117, 123–124, 128–129, 131, 134
  data collection and use, 117–118, 129, 132–133, 134–135, 137
  as echo chamber, 137
  high-impact journal publication, 124–126, 131
  information asymmetry in, 116, 129–130
  inherent bias in, 130–131, 136
  journals and impact factor, 124–126, 137
  library values endangered by, 117, 118, 134–135
  nature of innovation in, 121–122
  privacy concerns, 132–133, 134–135
  quantification of higher education, 128
  research impacts, 117, 118, 130–131
  surveillance publishing model, 117, 118, 130–131
  vendor lock-in, 134–135, 136
collections. *See* libraries
Collini, Stefan, 121, 125
commercial film streaming platforms.
  See also academic film streaming

platforms; streaming film platforms
- algorithms, data-determinism, and access, 76–79
- how we watch shaped by, 79
- library standards altered by, 75–76
- market power of, 71–72
- narrative and creative design shaped by, 79–80

costs and fees. *See also* capitalism; market capture
- gatekeeping information through, 16–17
- increases for libraries, 36–37, 41–42, 47, 50
- of platformization, 45, 46, 127–128, 132
- platform power and, 10–11

Cottom, Tressie McMillan, 135

Daniels, Heather, 134
data
- algorithms and access, 76–79
- collection and use, 51, 76–77, 117–118, 129, 132–135, 137
- data donation, 108
- Facebook–Cambridge Analytica data scandal, 92, 104
- as product, 116–117, 123–124, 128–129, 131, 134

#Datenspende, 108
Devoise, Marc, 77
digital heritage, 87–88
digital lending platforms. *See also* closed-loop academic publishing; Hoopla; Libby; OverDrive; streaming film platforms
- alternative platforms, 52–54
- asymmetric relationship with libraries, 38–40, 43
- business model, 38–39, 42
- case study methods, 32–33, 56–57
- chokepoints in lending ecosystem, 41
- contract law, 30
- cost increases for libraries, 36–37, 41–42, 47, 50
- digital rights management (DRM) software, 36–37, 42
- goal divergence between platforms and libraries, 29, 30, 39–40, 45, 51
- as intermediaries between publishers and libraries, 38
- librarians' advocacy for change to, 48–54
- librarians' loss of control over collections, 29–31, 35–36, 37, 41–42, 50, 54
- licensing over ownership of digital materials, 29–30, 35–36, 37–38, 42, 47
- market capture, 31–32, 38
- new property regime in digital collections, 30, 31, 35–36, 37–38
- patron identification with, 40
- privacy concerns, 46–48, 49, 52

Digital Public Library of America, 52–53
Disney+, 71–72
Doctorow, Cory, 41
Dougherty, Michael R., 131

Eaton, Charlie, 134
ebooks. *See* digital lending platforms; licensing
#ebookSOS, 50
eBook Study Group (New York University), 49
EBSCO, 128, 133
#econtentforlibraries, 50
Elsevier, 123, 124, 128, 133–134, 135
Engels, Frederich, 122
erotica, 28–29
Ex Libris, 131–132

Facebook
- application programming interfaces (APIs), 98, 103, 104
- web archiving of, 93, 94–95, 97–99

Facebook–Cambridge Analytica data scandal, 92, 104
Film and Medial Round Table, 82–83
films, 63, 64–66. *See also* streaming film platforms
Films on Demand/Films Media Group, 69

Ganter, Sarah Anne, 4–5, 8, 17, 63–64, 116, 129–130
Gates, Bill, 7
Giblin, Rebbecca, 14, 41
Gillespie, Tarleton, 4

Grosshopper Films, 70
Grossmann, Alexander, 127

Hachette Livre, 41
Halperin, Jennie Rose, 50–51
Hamilton, Laura T., 134
HarperCollins, 41
Haufe, Chris, 124
Helmond, Anne, 6–7, 90n13
higher education. *See also* closed-loop academic publishing
    artificial intelligence (AI) and, 123, 135–136
    critiques of, 119–120
    gamification of promotion processes, 125
    journals and impact factor, 124–126
    open access publishing, 127
    prestige and, 120–121, 125–126
    quantification of, 119–125, 126–127, 128
Hong, Sun-Ha, 122
Hoopla, 27–29, 41, 51

Illingworth, David, 131
information. *See also* data
    asymmetry in, 15–17, 116, 129–130
    as capitalist commodity, 6, 16–17, 116–117, 123–124, 128–129, 131, 134
    costs as gatekeeping of, 16–17
Instagram, 102, 104
Interfolio, 134
Internet Archive, 50, 88–89, 94
internet search, 6

Johnson, Sarah, 28–29, 32, 41–42, 44
journals. *See* closed-loop academic publishing; digital lending platforms

Kanopy, 47–48, 66, 69
KKR private equity firm, 42, 44
Knee, Jonathan, 70
Kweli.tv, 70

labour practices, 10
Lamdan, Sarah, 126, 131, 134
Lamphere, Carley, 68
Libby, 30, 44

libraries. *See also* capitalism; costs and fees; data; platformization; platforms; property
    advocacy for change, 48–54, 138–139
    biases of structures, 12
    chokepoints in lending ecosystem, 41
    commodification of information, 6
    as extensions of the state, 5–6
    film collections, 63, 64–66
    platform amalgamation, 13–14
    service mandate, 34–36
library and information studies (LIS), 11
Library Futures (New York University), 50–51
Library Services Platforms (LSP), 7
licensing
    for film collections, 73, 75, 80–81
    replacing digital ownership model, 29–30, 35–36, 37–38, 42, 47

Macmillan Publishers, 41
market capture
    academic publishing, 134–135, 136
    digital lending platforms, 31–32, 38
    resource control, 14
    streaming film platforms, 66–72
Mattern, Shannon, 136–137
Matthewman, Steve, 2
McCormick, Casey, 79–80
Meta, 117. *See also* Facebook; Instagram

National Library of Australia (NLA), 91–92, 93–99, 100–101, 105
Naxos, 69
Netflix, 71–72, 76–77, 79
Newfield, Christopher, 120
New York Public Library, 46
Nguyen, Rosalind, 131
Nieborg, David, 90n13
Nielsen, Rasmus Kleis, 4–5, 8, 17, 63–64, 116, 129–130
NLA. *See* National Library of Australia (NLA)
Noble, Safiya Umoja, 123n13

Olsen, Hope, 12
open access publishing, 127
OverDrive. *See also* Kanopy

asymmetric relationship with
  libraries, 43, 44, 45, 47–48
claim to serve libraries, 43, 44
content instability, 44
as Costco for libraries, 51
cost to libraries, 45, 46
digital lending chokepoints, 41
as intermediary between publishers
  and libraries, 43, 49
legal action, 49–50
Libby lending application, 30, 44
multiple library cards registered to a
  profile, 45–46
new property regime in digital
  collections, 30
ownership of, 42
privacy concerns, 46–48, 49, 52

Palace Project, 52–53
Parker, Carmi, 41–42, 43–44
Pasquale, Frank, 135
Penguin Random House, 41
Plantin, Jean-Christophe, 90
platformization
  author's overview, 6–8
  library goals and, 29, 30, 39–40, 45,
    51, 101, 105–106
  library standards endangered, 73–76
  library values endangered, 39–40,
    117, 118, 134–135
  private corporations' interests
    privileged, 107
  of the web, 89–90
platform power. See also capitalism;
  costs and fees; market capture;
  privacy
  global power, 10
  power of automated action at scale,
    13–14
  power of information asymmetry,
    15–17
  power to make or break
    connections, 11–13
  power to operate across domains,
    17–18
  power to set standards, 9–11
platforms. See also closed-loop
  academic publishing; digital lending
  platforms; market capture; social
media platforms; streaming film
platforms
  author's overview, 3–5
  bias in metadata, 12–13
  creators' worldviews and interests,
    influence of, 9–10
  diversity decreased by, 15–16
  as intermediaries, 38, 43, 49
  relationality of, 9
  technology of, 2–3
  touting importance of openness,
    16, *16*
  US lens dominating, 9–10
Poell, Thomas, 90n13
Pooley, Jeff, 130
Porter, Theodore, 119
Posada, Alejandro, 127
Potash, Steve, 43
Pragda, 70
privacy
  author's overview, 10
  campaigns around privacy concerns,
    51–52
  closed-loop academic publishing
    and, 132–133, 134–135
  digital lending platforms and, 46–48,
    49, 52
  eroded by technology of platforms, 3
  surveillance publishing model, 117,
    118, 130–131
private corporations, 14
ProctorU, 128
property, 30–38. See also digital lending
  platforms; licensing
ProQuest/Clarivate, 69, 128, 130, 131–132
publishing. See closed-loop academic
  publishing; digital lending platforms

Rakuten, 42
Readers First initiative, 45
Riegelhaupt, Kathleen, 46

Schlosberg, Justin, 4
Schonfeld, Roger, 134
Seeman, Dean, 11–12
Simon & Schuster, 41
Smith, Christian Michael, 134
Smith, Trista, 14
social media platforms

Index

application programming interfaces (APIs), 92–93, 98, 99–104
counter-archiving, 106–107
data as product, 117
data donation, 108
goal divergence with libraries, 101, 105–106
web archiving challenges, 90–92
web archiving of, 91–92, 93–99, 100–105
web crawling, 92, 93–99
Srnicek, Nick, 38–39
State Library of New South Wales (SLNSW), 91–92, 101–104, 105
St. Mary's County Library (Maryland), 45
streaming film platforms. *See also* academic film streaming platforms; commercial film streaming platforms
  author's overview, 63–64
  commercial streaming platforms, 67–69, 71–72, 75–80
  distribution and end-user agreements, 66–69
  long-term access and preservation, 80–83
  market dominance, 66–72
  supply-side scale, 69–71
Suber, Peter, 127
supply-side scale, 69–70. *See also* market capture
SVOD. *See* streaming film platforms
Swank Digital Campus, 69

Taylor, Jamie, 132
Twitter. *See* X (formerly Twitter)

Video Trust, 82–83

web archives and archiving. *See also* Internet Archive
  application programming interfaces (APIs), 92–93, 98, 99–101, 105–106
  counter-archiving, 106–107
  data donation, 108
  digital heritage and, 88–89
  platformization's challenges to, overview, 90–92, 105–106
  web crawling techniques, 92, 93–99

Whatcom County Library System (Washington), 43–44
Willimon, Beau, 79
Writers Guild of America (WGA), 71–72

X (formerly Twitter)
  application programming interfaces (APIs), 93n25, 100–101, 102, 103, 104
  data as product, 117
  web archiving of, 92–93, 95–97, *96*, *97*, 100–101

Ziskina, Juliya, 49–50

www.ingramcontent.com/pod-product-compliance
Lightning Source LLC
Chambersburg PA
CBHW050111170426
43198CB00014B/2540